JESUS OUR BROTHER

The Humanity of the Lord

WILFRID J. HARRINGTON, OP

Paulist Press
New York / Mahwah, NJ

Cover design by Sharyn Banks
Book design by Lynn Else

Library of Congress Cataloging-in-Publication Data

Harrington, Wilfrid J.
    Jesus our brother : the humanity of the Lord / Wilfrid J. Harrington.
        p. cm.
    Includes bibliographical references (p.   ).
    ISBN 978-0-8091-4671-0 (alk. paper)
    1. Jesus Christ—Humanity. I. Title.
    BT218.H37 2010
    232′.8—dc22

                                                                2010009884

Published by Paulist Press
997 Macarthur Boulevard
Mahwah, New Jersey 07430

www.paulistpress.com

Printed and bound in the
United States of America

CONTENTS

iii

Contents

PREFACE

"LET US RUN WITH perseverance the race that is set before us, looking to Jesus the pioneer and perfecter of our faith" (Hebrews 12:1–2). For the author of Hebrews, faith in Jesus, the High Priest seated "at the right hand of the throne of God" (12:2), is what gives meaning to the Christian way. At the same time, no other New Testament writer has stressed more than he the humanity of this heavenly high priest—for he has in sight a specific historical person: Jesus of Nazareth.

Yet, after New Testament times, what came to be was ahistorical Christology that displayed little of the vulnerable Jesus who died on a cross. Even when they have kept the earthly Jesus in view, people have tended to detach the death of Jesus from his life and his resurrection from his career and death. To do this is to ignore the challenge of the prophet Jesus and, ultimately, to fail to grasp the significance of his death and the true meaning of his resurrection. The life of Jesus of Nazareth is the key to what Christianity is all about. In the human *Jesus* we meet God. This is the astounding truth at the heart of Christianity.

This book is not an essay in Christology. Its purpose is modest and specific: I simply seek to illustrate the authentic humanity of Jesus of Nazareth by highlighting his characteristically human traits. It is necessary, however, to set them in proper context. There is his call to mission and how he would have seen himself, and how others would have regarded him. There are his concerns, his priorities. And there is the reaction of others to his person and to his vision.

As Son of God, Jesus had come to reveal the Father. They crucified him. God vindicated his Son by raising him from death. God's unfaithful children will not frustrate his saving purpose for them. That message of the Old Testament is verified in the life, death, and resurrection of Jesus of Nazareth.

INTRODUCTION

OUR CONCERN IS THE humanity of Jesus of Nazareth—the features that mark him firmly as one of us. Yet, the great Christian truth is that, in Jesus of Nazareth, God is really and truly present. His humanity is not the whole of it. The identity of Jesus is mystery in the strictest sense.[1] To seek to define the mysterious reality of Jesus was, and remains, a formidable theological challenge.

Here let us venture a modest sketch.

Image of the Invisible God

"Who do you say that I am?" (Mark 8:29). This challenging question put to the disciples at Caesarea Philippi is one that Christians have continued to face over the centuries. It may be argued that the earliest answers are still the best. One looks to Paul. His response rings with conviction: Jesus is "the image of the invisible God" (Col 1:15). The Fourth Gospel offers a relevant commentary: "No one has ever seen God. It is God the only Son, who is close to the Father's heart, who has made him known" (John 1:18). The transcendent, unknowable God is now visible and knowable in the incarnate Son: "the Word became flesh and lived among us" (1:14). And, throughout the Fourth Gospel, the role of the Son is Revealer of the Father. The author of Hebrews makes his contribution: "Long ago God spoke to our ancestors in many and various ways by the prophets, but in these last days he has spoken to us by a Son....He is the reflection of God's glory and the exact imprint of God's very being" (1:1–3). God had indeed spoken in the scriptures of Israel, and continues to speak to us there. But there is now, besides, a definitive word, a word not uttered or written, a word that is *person*, the Son. And this person, who reflects God's glory and carries the imprint of the very reality of God, "had to be like his brothers and sisters in every respect...tested as we are," sharing "our flesh and blood" (2:17; 4:15; 2:14). Jesus is divine indeed, with a divinity that finds whole expression in a full humanity. Put more simply, Jesus is the human person in whom God is wholly present.

If Jesus bears the stamp of God's very being, he does so as a human person, like us in all things. *Jesus* tells us what God is like. *Jesus* is God's summons to us, God's challenge to us. In Jesus God has shown himself in human form—"he is the image of the invisible God" (Col 1:15). In practice, we have slipped quickly past this human aspect. We have turned instead to a "divine icon" comfortably free of any trait of the critical prophet. We have consigned Jesus to his heavenly home—and wisely, because we realized a long time ago that he is safer there! We genuflect before "our divine Lord" who does not impinge on us because of how we envisage him. He really has no critical impact on the life of our world. But Jesus of Nazareth is a very uncomfortable person to have about. There stands the gospel and its challenge, its "dangerous memory."

The mystery of Jesus is that in him, God communicates himself in a full and unrestricted manner: "In him all the fullness of God was pleased to dwell" (Col 1:19). Jesus' divinity is not, as sometimes presented, a kind of second substance in him. His divinity lies in the fact that, as the perfect counterpart of God, he is the manifestation and presence of God in our world. When the human Jesus is not acknowledged, our understanding of God suffers, and our Christianity suffers. "The gospel is good news not just about Jesus but about the God of Jesus, the maker of heaven and earth, the God of all men and women....We Christians learn to express stammeringly the content of what 'God' is, and the content of what 'humanity' can be, from the career of Jesus."[2]

Jesus Christ

The object of Christian faith is the person of Jesus Christ who briefly lived in the first century AD and now lives on in the Father's presence. The subject of our gospels is this Jesus Christ. The gospels, at once historical and theological, proclaim Jesus of Nazareth as the Christ, the definitive revelation of God. The Jesus they proclaim is a construct of Christian theological and spiritual imagination aimed at eliciting a faith response. The proclamation embraces strictly historical elements (Jesus' death on the cross, for example) and theological interpretation in terms of biblical categories (for example, his ascent to God's right hand).

The real or actual Jesus is the glorified Savior in our midst. He will always be shrouded in mystery. The total reality of any person is unknowable to human discernment—how much more the reality of the Risen One. The gospels present us with "the earthly Jesus": a portrait of Jesus during his life on earth. This partial, theologically colored picture serves as the source for the theoretical construct, "the historical Jesus." The historical Jesus is not the real Jesus but only a fragmentary reconstruction of him by modern means of research. But this reconstruction is of immense importance, particularly in our day. Jesus is an appealing and a challenging figure.[3]

The historical Jesus is not coextensive with the Jesus of the gospel narratives, for there is much in them that is not historical. The gospel picture is "accurate," not in the sense that it is exact in detail, but that it is truth-bearing. It is the acceptance of this picture by the early believing community that guarantees the substantial truth of the gospel account. The gospel Jesus is more than the historical Jesus: the gospel presents not only history but the trans-historical, not only fact but theological interpretation.

Gospel

Gospel is not a wholly distinctive literary form. It belongs to a broad Greco-Roman genre of *bioi*—lives—or, more specifically, historical "lives." The purpose of a *bios* was, above all, to bring out clearly the nature of the subject. A gospel, as a *bios Iésou* (life of Jesus), highlights the uniqueness of Jesus in terms of Christology. Our gospels are a mixture of narrative and discourse, centered on the person, life, and teaching of Jesus of Nazareth, with special interest in his death and resurrection. All four evangelists were concerned to set out both the *story* of Jesus as well as what they took to be the *significance* of *his* activity and teaching, and their bearing on Christian life. He is the focus; he gives meaning to all.

A *gospel* is not objective biography; this story is shot through with resurrection faith. A *gospel* is written for believers: it is a Christian document addressed to Christians. More specifically, each gospel was, in the first place, written for a particular Christian community and with the needs of that community firmly in mind. The evangelists presented the "facts" with the intention of bringing out the meaning that the events held for those who encountered them. They set out to voice the faith of the early church. The nucleus of that faith is that the crucified Jesus had been raised from the dead.

The fourth evangelist shows us the aim of an evangelist. The purpose of his selective presentation of the "signs" of Jesus was in order that the Christian disciple might go on believing that the historical person, Jesus, is the Messiah of Jewish expectation, that he is the Son of God. He wrote so that, through their deepened faith in Jesus Christ, Christians might find life in him and live that life to the full (John 20:31). In other words, his concern was Christology and discipleship. The gospels are proclamations of the Good News. They are aimed at Christians striving to live the Christian Way.

Our study of the humanity of Jesus is based on these gospels. It will quickly become apparent that Mark's story will figure most prominently. This for two reasons: It is broadly accepted that Mark is our earliest Gospel; more significantly, Mark's Jesus is the most human in the gospels.

Jesus of Nazareth

Jesus of Nazareth was a Jew of the first century AD who began, lived, and ended his short life in a minor province of the Roman Empire. Our information about him is meager by historical standards. Apart from two brief statements by the Jewish historian Flavius Josephus and the Roman historian Tacitus, our sources for knowledge of the historical Jesus are the canonical gospels alone. We really know nothing precise about the life of Jesus before the start of his mission. The infancy narratives of Matthew and Luke are primarily christological texts, and they are not in total agreement. They tell us that Jesus was, most likely, born in Bethlehem during the reign of Herod the Great. They all assert that Jesus was brought up in Nazareth of Galilee. Later, he was known as "the Nazarene." A summary of the historical facts about Jesus of Nazareth, based on the meticulous research of a major New Testament scholar, will serve our purpose.[4]

Around 7–4 BC, that is, toward the close of the reign of Herod the Great, a Jewish boy, to be named Jesus (Yeshua), was born in Bethlehem of Judea. His mother was named Mary (Miryam) and his putative father Joseph (Yosef). He grew up in Nazareth and was known as "the Nazarene." His native tongue was Aramaic; he would have had a practical command of Greek. It is highly likely that he was literate; as a boy he would have been taught in the village synagogue. Like Joseph (Matt 13:55), Jesus (Mark 6:3) was a *tektón*, an artisan—most probably, a carpenter. He would have learned his craft from Joseph as an apprentice.

Jesus was a layman who lived in the quiet obscurity of a Galilean village. It is not surprising that the gospels (outside the passion narratives) show no evidence of any dealings with the Jerusalem priests. They would have had no interest in a Galilean layman—until they began to perceive him as a threat. The Letter to the Hebrews does, of course, elaborate a theology of the priesthood of Christ. It is precisely that: a theological construct—the heavenly priesthood of the Risen One. The author is perfectly aware that the earthly Jesus was not a priest: "Now if he were on earth, he would not be a priest at all, since there are priests who offer gifts according to the law" (8:4); "It is evident that our

Lord was descended from Judah, and in connection with that tribe Moses said nothing about priests" (7:14).

In our modern world we have a fascination with dates and times—birthdays, and so on. When one really thinks about it, such precision is of little importance. I was born; I will die—this is the reality that is mightily important to me. Marks on a calendar are of little significance. It matters little that we are unable to date precisely the birth, mission, and death of Jesus. We may, at best, propose a fair approximation:

Birth	7–6 BC.
Beginning of mission	AD 28. If Jesus began his mission early in 28, it would have lasted a little over two years.
Death	AD 30, 14 Nisan—eve of Passover. Jesus would have been about 36 at his death.

1

JESUS OF NAZARETH: LIFE

Nazareth

NAZARETH WAS A SMALL village, with a likely population of between 300 and 400, in southern Galilee, territory of Herod Antipas. It was an agricultural community of subsistence farmers. Joseph, Mary, and Jesus belonged to this peasant world, in the lower artisan class. In Roman times Galilean villagers were triply taxed: the traditional tithe for the support of the Jerusalem temple and priesthood; tribute to the Roman emperor; taxes to the local client-king, Antipas. This severe tax burden amounted to exploitation. Besides, there was the extra demand for the rebuilding of Sepphoris and the founding of Tiberias. Payment of taxes often involved borrowing that could lead to land being confiscated by creditors. Former farmers or tenant farmers could end up as day laborers or beggars. This socioeconomic situation might, as we shall see, have influenced the later conduct and preaching of Jesus.

It has been suggested that the rebuilding of Sepphoris, less than four miles from Nazareth, may have been to the advantage of the village. "Its proximity to a city reduced transport costs and made it profitable to grow the high-value labor-intensive perishable garden crops that were indispensable to the markets of Sepphoris. The city in return provided the villagers with employment as well as with goods and services not available at home. It was there they paid taxes and used courts and the banks (Matt 25:27)—and heard news of a wider world."[1] The rebuilding and settlement would have occurred during the boyhood and youth of Jesus. Sepphoris, though basically a Jewish city, was strongly marked by Hellenistic culture. In such close proximity to the town, Jesus could not have been unaware of another world, a lifestyle very different from that of his home village.

The religious life of Nazareth was solidly Jewish. Jesus belonged to an observant household that lived out their faith in the one God of Israel in the rounds of ordinary daily life, in sabbath rest, and in prayer. Synagogue meant, most likely, more a village assembly than a building exclusively for religious purpose—the Greek word *synagógé* means an assembly or a congregation of people. The anchors of religious life were the family household and the public assembly, notably on the sabbath. There was also pilgrimage to Jerusalem. This must have been occasional because families under such severe economic stress could not readily take off on the three or so weeks needed for the journey. Later, Jesus, as itinerant preacher, would have wider scope.

The Forerunner

In all four gospels, before the mission of Jesus opens, John the Baptist is introduced. According to the synoptic gospels (not, however, in the Fourth Gospel), Jesus was baptized by John. Who is this John? In his *Jewish Antiquities* the Jewish historian Flavius Josephus tells of the execution of John by Herod Antipas. He has it in the context of the defeat of Herod by the Nabatean king Aretas IV in AD 26. He describes John, surnamed the Baptist, as one who baptized Jews who "were cultivating virtue and practicing justice toward one another and piety toward God." Because John had a notable following, Herod feared that his popularity might spark a revolt. He decided on a preemptive strike and had John arrested and sent in chains to Machaerus, a fortress south of the Dead Sea. This account of the death of the Baptist is preferable to the evidently legendary story of Mark 6:17–29.

It is clear from the text of Josephus (and he has more to say of the Baptist than of Jesus) that John had been a prominent figure. This is borne out by the gospels. Paradoxically, they witness to the importance of the Baptist by consistently cutting him down to size. In Mark (1:2–11) the Baptizer is he who would prepare the way for "one who is more powerful than I." He was unaware that Jesus was that mighty one. In Matthew (3:13–15) John recognized Jesus' status and acknowledged his own inferiority. In Luke (1:41–44; 3:19–21) Jesus met with his cousin John. It is not explicitly stated that he was baptized by John; the implication is there. In the Fourth Gospel John is not given the title *Baptist*—there is an oblique reference to his practice of baptizing (1:25–26). There is no place for the baptism of Jesus by John. Here the raison d'être of John is to witness to Jesus (John 1:7–8, 19, 23, 29, 34; 3:29–30).

It is evident that early Christians were increasingly uneasy at this baptism of the Lord by the Baptist— embarrassment is evident in Matthew 3:13–14. The reaction underlines the firm historicity of the occurrence: They were stuck with the fact. The matter is complicated by the characterization of John's baptism as "a baptism of repentance for the forgiveness of sins" (Mark 1:4). This made Jesus' submission to John's baptism even more problematic. In Jesus' estimation, however, his baptism was not only a sign of the candidates' repentance but a pledge of new life, of a radical change. It was, too, symbolically, an anticipation of an ultimate total cleansing of sin. In this perspective, a Jesus who was not conscious of sin could accept baptism from John.

John, in short, emerges as an eschatological prophet: He proclaimed the imminence of the end, marked by fiery judgment. This is a distinctively apocalyptic view. From the apocalyptic perspective there is, in our world, a war to the death between good and evil. Good will surely triumph. Evil, and all evildoers, will perish in a final conflagration. Now is the time of decision. The tone of the Baptist's clarion call (in Matthew and Luke) is characteristic of apocalyptic: "You brood of vipers! Who warned you to flee from the wrath to come? ...Even now the ax is lying to the root of the trees...every tree that does not bear good fruit is cut down and thrown into the fire...his winnowing fork is in his hand...; the chaff he will burn with unquenchable fire" (Matt 3:10–12; see Luke 3:7–9). The evidence, from Josephus and the gospels (see Matt 11:2–29; Luke 7:18–35), substantiates the impression that John the Baptist, a Jewish prophet, had gained a reputation and a following. For very different reasons he attracted the attention of Herod Antipas and of Jesus of Nazareth. His ministry preceded that of Jesus—who indeed became involved in it for a time. And this movement did not end with John's death but continued apart from the Christian movement (see Acts 18:24—19:7).

Disciple of the Baptist

The starting point for any account of the mission of Jesus of Nazareth is his encounter with John the Baptist, the call that Jesus heard when he was baptized by John and to which he responded. By submitting to baptism Jesus became, in effect, a disciple of the Baptist.[2] Jesus the *tektón* had, presumably, learned his trade from Joseph. It is quite in the human way that the prophet Jesus had been apprenticed to a prophet. There is the biblical precedent of Elijah and Elisha (1 Kings 19:19–21; 2 Kings 2:13–18). Significantly, the Baptist appears in the gospels as an Elijah figure (see Mark 1:6; 9:9–13). John had begun his mission in the wilderness (Luke 3:2) of Perea, beyond the Jordan, appearing where Elijah had disappeared (2 Kings 2) and forcing the question of his identity (Mark 1:6). A wilderness audience would be Galilean pilgrims, avoiding hostile Samaria in a roundabout way to Jerusalem (see Luke 9:51–53). Jesus, very likely, had heard of this prophet. Now, as a Galilean pilgrim, he encountered this strange and striking man, dressed in a camel-hair cloak bound with a leather belt: an Elijah figure. Jesus received baptism and stayed with John, as Elisha had become a disciple of Elijah. Later, some of John's disciples, whether or not at his instigation, transferred to Jesus (John 1:35–42).

Some statements in the Fourth Gospel imply much more than might appear at first sight. Take John 3:22–23: "After this Jesus and his disciples went into the Judean countryside, and he spent some time there with them and baptized. John was also baptizing at Aenon near Salim [in Samaria]." We could take this to mean that John had sent Jesus into Judea, while he had gone to the more challenging Samaria. That the ministry of Jesus, at this stage, involved baptism is explicit in 3:22 and 4:1—"Now when Jesus had heard, 'Jesus is making and baptizing more disciples than John....' " The observation reflects a later dispute as to the relative merits of John's and Jesus' ministry. It is obvious that 4:2—"although it was not Jesus himself but his disciples who baptized"—is a maladroit redactional "correction." Evidently, the concern was to distance Jesus from the Baptist. The simple situation was that, as disciple, Jesus, like his master, "proclaimed a baptism of repentance for the forgiveness of sins" (see Mark 1:4).

Later, John moved into Galilee, territory of Herod Antipas, and was promptly arrested. The observation in John 4:3 is significant: "[Jesus] left Judea and started back to Galilee." The Baptist had been silenced. Jesus moved in to take his place. What emerges from all this is that, at first, Jesus was disciple of, and in the line of, the Baptist. Then came a radical change in the pattern of Jesus' activity. He ceased to baptize and proclaimed a different message. It was no longer the Baptist's word of woe and clarion call to "Repent!" Jesus now proclaimed: "The kingdom of God has come near" (Mark 1:15). Where John proclaimed the judgment of God, Jesus proclaimed the salvation of God. Hearing, in prison, of this new turn, a perplexed John sent two of his disciples to investigate. Jesus' response was: "Go and tell John what you have seen and heard: the blind receive their sight, the lame walk, the lepers are cleansed, the deaf hear, the dead are raised, the poor have good news brought to them" (Luke 7:22). One can read between the lines. John was being told that there was another prophetic message, another prophetic style. One might put it that John was in the line of Amos—that prophet of unrelieved gloom. Jesus was in the line of Hosea, prophet of God's gracious love (see Hosea 1—3; 11). We must not, however, overlook the fact that Jesus, like Hosea, spoke words of warning.

Prophet—Teacher—Healer

PROPHET

In the Bible a prophet is God's spokesperson, one called and sent to proclaim the word of God. Old Testament prophets were very conscious of the call and of the task. We see this clearly when we look at an Amos, a Hosea, an Isaiah, a Jeremiah. "The Lord took me from following the flock....And the Lord said to me, 'Go, prophesy to my people Israel' " (Amos 7:15); "Then I heard the voice of the Lord, saying, 'Whom shall I send?' ...And I said, 'here I am, send me!' " (Isa 6:8); "Before I formed you in the womb I knew you....I appointed you a prophet to the nations" (Jer 1:5). The call was a powerful summons; the task was challenging and formidable. There was need for commitment and courage. By and large, the prophetic word would not be heard. The task involved suffering and rejection—even death. Jeremiah is a poignant instance of the loneliness of the call: "Under the weight of your hand I sat alone" (Jer 15:7). The mysterious prophetical figure of Second Isaiah paid the price in vicarious suffering: "He was despised and rejected. He was wounded for our transgressions...yet he bore the sin of many and made intercession for the transgressors" (Isa 53:3–12).

Jesus of Nazareth was a prophet. As one who spoke—who was!—God's definitive word (see Heb 1:2), he was the eschatological prophet. As "image of the invisible God" (Col 1:15), everything he did and said was manifestation of God. Jesus had served his prophetical apprenticeship under John the Baptist. His decision to launch his distinctive mission was based on his consciousness of a unique relationship with his Abba. He knew himself to be one called and sent: "I must proclaim the good news of the kingdom of God...for I was sent for this purpose" (Luke 4:43). The kingdom, the rule of God, is, in the long run, God himself as salvation of humankind. Salvation reaches into every aspect of human life. As with Elijah and Elisha, healing was part of Jesus' prophetic mission. This is explicit in his inaugural program (Luke 4:14–30).

Coming to his Nazareth synagogue on a sabbath, Jesus was invited to take the scripture reading. He opened the scroll of Isaiah and read out:

> The Spirit of the Lord is upon me,
> because he has anointed me to bring good news to
>   the poor.
> He has sent me to proclaim release to the captives
> and recovery of sight to the blind,
> to let the oppressed go free,
> to proclaim the year of the Lord's favor.
>
> (Luke 4:18–19)

He had taken care to close his reading before the next phrase of the Isaian passage—"and the day of the vengeance of our God" (Isa 61:2). "Vengeance" would be no part of his message. Then he declared: "Today this scripture has been fulfilled in your hearing" (Luke 4:21). This, then, is Jesus' program as he embarks on his mission. His program: good news to the poor...freedom of captives... relief of the oppressed. What is this but a form of liberation theology!

Jesus of Nazareth had responded to the challenge of an uncompromising prophet: John the Baptist. He became a prophet in his turn and began to proclaim the good news of the rule of God: "The time is fulfilled, and the kingdom of God has come near" (Mark 1:15). The precise phrase *kingdom of God* occurs only once in the Old Testament, in Wisdom 10:10. The expression was not current at the time of Jesus and was not widely used by early Christians. "Kingdom of God" is found predominantly in the synoptics and then almost always on the lips of Jesus. It was evidently central to Jesus' proclamation. Israel regarded God as universal king. And there was the expectation that God's reign would soon be manifested over the whole world. This is why "reign" or "rule" of God is a more satisfactory rendering of the Aramaic *malkutha di' elaha*. "Kingdom of God" is, however, traditionally firmly in place.

Jesus spoke, in the main, of a future kingdom: God will reveal himself in power and glory. There is evidence that Jesus also spoke of the kingdom as in some way already present in his own words and deeds. When we have in mind the fact that "kingdom of God" is not primarily a state or place, but rather the dynamic event of God coming in power to rule his people Israel in the end-time, it is not surprising that the precise relationship between a future and a present kingdom is not specified. That is why Jesus can speak of the kingdom as both imminent and yet present. In Jesus' eyes, his healings and exorcisms were part of the eschatological drama that was already being played out and on which God was about to bring down the curtain. The important point is that Jesus deliberately chose to proclaim that the display of miraculous power throughout his ministry was a preliminary and partial realization of God's kingly rule.

God's rule becomes real only when it finds expression in human life. It found expression in the life of Jesus. He "went about, doing good"; he championed the outcast; he welcomed sinners. Jesus, in his own lifestyle, gave concrete expression to the good life—a life worthy of humankind. It is up to us, his disciples, to give concrete expression, in our turn, to the good life. It is our task to give the kingdom flesh and blood in our world. Of course, the kingdom that would emerge if God's rule were to hold sway would be very different from any existing political entity, and different, too, from any religious structure then and now.

The kingdom can be a reality only at the cost of whole-hearted conversion. It is the charism of a prophet to see to the heart of things. Only the starkest words can match his uncomplicated vision. The genuine prophet will speak a message of comfort, based on the faithfulness of God, but it will never be a comfortable message. That is why the demands of Jesus were uncompromising. He knew, better than any other, that sin was the greatest evil, the ultimate slavery. He discerned sin in selfishness and greed, in the seeking of status—most reprehensibly in the seeking of ecclesiastical power and privilege. He was conscious of sinful structures, political and religious. Indeed, he turned authority upside down (Mark 10:42–45). He took his stand on the Fatherhood/Motherhood of God. He believed that all men and women are children of this Parent, that all are sisters and brothers. He regarded sin as whatever conflicts with that family relationship of respect and love. Logically, then, his prophetic message was "good news for the poor." The poor are victims of the oppressive power of sin, an oppression mediated through sinful structures. This concern of Old Testament prophets found fresh urgency in Jesus' preaching.

In preaching the rule of God, Jesus was defining God. He proclaimed a God bent on the salvation of humankind. That is why he announced good news to the poor—the needy of every sort, the outcast. That is why he was friend of sinners, why he had table fellowship with them. And, in the long run, it was because Jesus had proclaimed a God of over-whelming mercy that he ended up on a cross. That God was unacceptable to the religious people of his day. That God is unacceptable to the professionally religious of any day.

TEACHER

In Jesus the roles of prophet and teacher overlapped. If he was in the tradition of the prophets of Israel, he was also in the tradition of the sages of Israel. He transcended their role also. They were persuasive. He displayed another quality: "They were astounded at his teaching, because he spoke with authority" (Luke 4:32). Another quality indeed because his *exousia* (authority) carried no trace of domi-neering. He could tell his disciples: "I am among you as one who serves" (22:26). The authority of his teaching lay in the fact that his words were healing words, saving words. He would exhort his disciples: "Be merciful, just as your Father is merciful" (6:36).

As a first-century Palestinian Jew he, of course, shared much of the theology of his tradition. But there was more than enough to set him apart. The ultimate fact was his understanding of God. Clashes with his religious oppo-nents over matters of laws, such as sabbath observance, were symptomatic of fundamental difference. Jesus knew, better than any other, that to proclaim one's belief in God is not enough. What matters, and matters utterly, is the kind of God in whom one believes. It makes, literally, a world of difference whether one's God is the true God or a distorted image of that God. For Jesus, God is God of humankind. God is found where there is goodness and a striving for the liberation of humankind. We are human beings, created in the image of God. Our destiny is to be human—as God understands "human." The corollary is that only with God can we reach full humanity. Jesus, with God, reached whole humanity.

Here, it is widely believed, is where religion comes in. Religion, generally perceived as an area of humankind's relation with God, is, ostensibly, a system and manner of life that unites us with God, that enables us to be godly. Like all things human, religion is subject to corruption. The temptation of the religious person is to identify one's man-made world with the world of God and claim control over the holy. In practice, religion may be a barrier to creative union with God; it may lock us into a narrow impoverished way. Jesus uttered his word, at once criterion and critique: "The sabbath was made for humankind, and not humankind for the sabbath" (Mark 2:27). Here, "sabbath" is code for "religion," so the statement runs: "Religion is in the service of men and women; men and women are not slaves of religion." This is, perhaps, the most radical pronouncement of Jesus. It casts a cold eye on religion. Wherever religion is burden, wherever it shows lack of respect for human freedom, it has become oppressor, not servant. Authentic religion must foster freedom. Of course, one has to understand freedom correctly. In a Christian context, freedom is never license to do as one pleases. Paradoxically, the ultimate freedom is freedom to serve. "The Son of Man came not to be served but to serve, and to give his life as a ransom for many [all]" (10:45). Here is the sure christological basis of freedom.

As Teacher, Jesus had an eschatological perspective indeed—but he was deeply concerned with life in the here and now. He sought to reform Israel: He desired the fabric of life in his day to be transformed. Jesus had a refreshingly realistic understanding of salvation. Salvation happens in our world, in our history. Salvation comes from God but happens, as it must, in the lives of human beings. It reaches into and touches every aspect of human life. Otherwise it would not be salvation of humankind. Salvation is not confined within the confines of religion. Indeed, too often, religion is and has been an obstacle to salvation—the whole liberation of the wholly human. And it is only when men and women are free to be truly human that the human person becomes the image of God. It is only so that the true being of God may be revealed. Being image of God is not only the reflection of but also the revelation of God. Jesus of Nazareth is supremely the image of God. He is, transparently, the one "like his brothers and sisters in every respect" who is, at the same time and in his sheer humanity, "the reflection of God's glory and the exact imprint of God's very being" (Heb 2:17; 1:3). His teaching truly revealed God and the ways of God because of who he was.

Jesus offers no soft option. Christians may be children of God but only on condition that they understand what this means and live what it demands. The manner of being a child of God has been firmly traced: "Anyone who wants to be a follower of mine must renounce self, take up one's cross, and follow me" (Mark 8:34). Jesus delivered a challenge, the challenge of his own way as Son. Yet, taking up one's cross is not at all to say that suffering is something Christians should seek. Jesus did not seek suffering; Gethsemane is clear enough. But suffering will be part of Christian life as it was part of Jesus' life. The comfort is that following can be in modest steps. God is patient. His challenge is invitation. Faithfulness to one's way of life, concern for others in whatever manner, the caring gesture, the kind word—these add up. The Lord does not overlook the painful decision, the unspoken sorrow, the secret suffering. Jesus showed profound understanding of, and keen sympathy with, all aspects of the human lot.

HEALER

All four gospels agree that Jesus worked miracles—not just a few, but many. In the modern world, many find it difficult to accommodate the notion of miracle; many reject the possibility of miracle. In contrast, in the Greco-Roman world of Jesus' day, miracles were readily acknowledged. If Jesus did perform miracles, they would be accepted as such by his contemporaries. The majority of his miracles were healings of various diseases. His healing activity was motivated not only by his concern for suffering, his sympathy with the afflicted. It was also a sign of the in-breaking of the kingdom. The saving power of God was making its way into men's and women's lives.

Prominent among Jesus' miraculous deeds were exorcisms. It should be noted, first of all, that in the world of his day, illness was attributed to the invasion of evil forces. Healing could readily be envisaged as the "exorcizing" of the evil force. Take, for instance, the healing of Simon's mother-in-law. In Mark 1:31 Jesus "came and took her by the hand and lifted her up. Then the fever left her." He had healed her. In the parallel passage in Luke 4:39 we read: "Then he stood over her and rebuked the fever, and it left her"—a "rebuke" of the evil force. The healing in Mark has, by Luke, been transformed into an exorcism!

This aspect (exorcism) of Jesus' activity can and does upset our modern sensibility. The situation is aggravated by theatrical exploitation of the subject and by quite harmful interventions of would-be "exorcists." In the world of Jesus, on the other hand, exorcism was readily accepted both in paganism and in Judaism. It is, then, to be expected rather than come as a surprise that Jesus figured as an exorcist. John P. Meier comments:

> However disconcerting it may be to modern sensibilities, it is fairly certain that Jesus was, among other things, a first-century Jewish exorcist, and probably won not a little of his fame and following by practicing exorcisms....Perhaps in no other aspect of Jesus' ministry does his distance from modern Western culture and scientific technology loom so large and the facile program of making the historical Jesus instantly relevant to present-day men and women seem so ill-conceived. One can approach his exorcisms with greater sympathy if one remembers that Jesus no doubt saw them as part of his overall ministry of healing and liberating the people of Israel from the illnesses and other spiritual evils that beset them. Granted the primitive state of medical knowledge in the first-century Mediterranean world, mental illness, psychosomatic diseases, and such afflictions as epilepsy were often attributed to demonic possession. If Jesus saw himself called to battle against these evils, which diminished the lives of his fellow Israelites, it was quite natural for him, as a first-century Jew, to understand this specific dimension of his ministry in terms of exorcism. All of this

simply underscores the obvious: Jesus was a man and a Jew of his times.[3]

An obvious corollary is that a twenty-first-century Jesus would view the situation very differently; he would not be an exorcist. We must adjust our perspective to a first-century worldview.

SON OF MAN

Jesus had seen himself as a prophet and, it is likely, also as a sage. It is unlikely that he ever claimed to be the Messiah. It is, however, likely that Jesus' opponents may have understood him and his followers to claim that he was the Messiah. After the resurrection, of course, Jesus was, by his followers, regularly named the Messiah—Jesus Christ (Messiah). But he was a paradoxical Messiah: one who suffered, and died on a cross—not the triumphant royal messiah of popular expectation.

The term *Son of Man* occurs more than eighty times in the gospels and, practically without exception, as a self-designation by Jesus. He, however, never set out the meaning of the phrase, nor was it ever used to identify him. The expression itself is a literal rendering of the Aramaic idiom *bar 'enasha*, meaning "human being." Jesus used the phrase in a neutral sense to refer to himself indirectly, in the sense of our "one," implying the limitations of his humanness. Not unlikely, he had in mind as well the "one like a son of man" of Daniel 7:13, who had a vindication-following-suffering role. Jesus was the human one, serving God's purpose and looking to vindication at the conclusion of his mission. Early Christians embraced the phrase, now regarded as a title.

The Cross

The scandal of Jesus' death remains. Paul had had to wrestle with it. He has a name for divine logic: foolishness (see 1 Cor 1:22–25). If, as a Jew, he had to struggle painfully with the obduracy of Israel, the people's refusal to acknowledge their Messiah (see Romans 9—11), he had, again as a Jew, earlier come to terms with a deeper problem: that of a crucified Messiah. In Galatians he declared: "Christ redeemed us from the curse of the law by becoming a curse for us—for it is written, 'Cursed be everyone who hangs on a tree' " (3:13). There he adverts to what, for any Jew, would seem to be a fatal rebuttal of the Christian claim that Jesus was Messiah. There was the contrary evidence of Torah, the unambiguous word of Deuteronomy 21:22–23: "When someone is convicted of a crime punishable by death and is executed, his corpse must not remain all night upon the tree; you shall bury him that same day, for anyone hung on a tree is under God's curse."

In Christian tradition, Jesus had been duly condemned to death by the high priest and Sanhedrin as a "blasphemer" (Mark 14:63–64). And he had been "hung on a tree"—crucified. Manifestly abandoned by God, he could not, by any logic, be God's Anointed One. It is evident that Paul who had, consequently, been "a persecutor of the church" (Phil 3:6; see Gal 1:14, 23) in face of the outrageous Christian claim, had had, himself, to come to terms with the "scandal."

Paul, then, was acutely conscious of the formidable difficulty at the heart of the Christian message. If, at Caesarea Philippi, the reaction of Peter to the very suggestion that the Messiah might suffer was indignant rejection (Mark 8:31–33), how much more unacceptable for any Jew to acknowledge as Messiah one whom God had abandoned to a shameful death. As for the non-Jew: it was asking too much to recognize a savior in that hapless victim on a cross. When Paul declared, "We preach Christ crucified, a stumbling-block to Jews and folly to Gentiles" (1 Cor 1:23), he spoke from experience. He not only thought of the missionary challenge but, surely, recalled his personal conflict. He will not compromise. He wanted to know nothing "except Jesus Christ and him crucified" (2:2) because it was just here he had come to discern the power and the wisdom of God (see 1:24). Nor does Paul view the resurrection of Jesus as a "saving operation"; he would regard resurrection as inherent in the Cross.

The resurrection showed up the Cross in its true light and demonstrated that "God's foolishness is wiser than human wisdom, and God's weakness is stronger than human strength" (1:25). Paul would not draw a veil over the scandal of the cross. He would not argue with the foolishness of God. And God's "foolishness" was most manifest in his raising of Jesus from death.

"God proves his love for us in that while we still were sinners Christ died for us" (Rom 5:8). In Jesus of Nazareth the divine has entered into our history. God has become one among us. If Jesus bears the stamp of God's very being, he does so as a human person, like us in all things. Jesus shows us what God is like. Jesus is God's summons to us, God's challenge to us. We can say, truly, that God is love; we have no idea what divine love is in itself. In Jesus we see God's love in action. We learn that God is a God who is with us in our suffering and in our death. We are sure of it because of the suffering and death of Jesus. And we learn that God's gracious love truly has the last word.

2

JESUS OF NAZARETH: CONCERNS

JESUS ALWAYS PUT PEOPLE first. And his concern was, emphatically, for the vulnerable, the despised, and the outcast. He displayed special regard for those characterized as sinners.

The Poor

Jesus of Nazareth had a free attitude toward property. He took for granted the owning of property. In the setting of his Galilean village background, property would be modest indeed. He himself was a *tektón*, an artisan (Mark 6:3)—not a well-paid technician of our day, but a village tradesman. When he began his ministry and had abandoned his trade, he was supported, in his itinerant mission, by well-to-do women disciples (Luke 8:2–3). He urged that aged parents should be supported out of their children's means (Mark 7:9–10) and, in general, recommended that possessions be used to help the needy (12:41–42). In asking that money be lent without hope of return (Matt 5:42), Jesus was presupposing surplus funds that could be lent. The chief tax collector Zacchaeus was prepared to give half his possessions to the poor (Luke 10:8–9).

Jesus was invited to dinner by the rich and privileged (Luke 7:36; 14:1, 12). In the parable of the laborers in the vineyard he has the employer declare: "Am I not allowed to do what I choose with what belongs to me?" (Matt 20:15). While all of this may not, as such, go back in detail to Jesus himself, there is a pattern that surely is true to his attitude.

On the other hand, Jesus himself, during his itinerant mission, had no possessions. And he did, with severity, attack wealth where it had captured peoples' hearts and had blinded their eyes to God's purpose. He had surplus wealth especially in mind: The rich ought to use their wealth to benefit the poor. He was conscious of the difficulty of the challenge. An aspect of the saying, "It is easier for a camel to go through the eye of a needle than for someone who is rich to enter the kingdom of God" (Mark 10:25), is that it expresses the real difficulty the rich have of freeing themselves of possessions.

In dealing with wealth, Jesus does not suggest that wealth is evil in itself, independently of the disposition it may engender. Wealth is a misfortune when it not only makes one indifferent to the good of the future life but, too, when it distracts the rich from concern for the poor. It also tends to foster in the rich a feeling of security incompatible with that trust which God claims for himself alone. The admonition "Where your treasure is, there your heart will be also" (Luke 12:34) puts the matter in a nutshell. If one's heart is set on the kingdom (v. 31), then one will have the right perspective.

Jesus knew it to be his vocation to proclaim the true God—the Father. He knew that in faithfulness to his task he was making present the rule of God—God as salvation for humankind. That rule—the "kingdom"—has to be a reality among men and women already in the here and now. And he was making God's gracious power present not only in his healings and overcoming of evil, but also in his concern for the poor. How he saw his task is vividly portrayed in Luke's introduction of Jesus' mission (4:16–21). In his programmatic statement Jesus pointed to the recipients of his good news: captives, blind, oppressed—all who are weakest and powerless. They are "the poor." Albert Nolan strikingly characterizes Jesus as a social revolutionary:

> He turned the world, both Jewish and Gentile, upside down. This does not mean that Jesus was a typical revolutionary in the political sense of the word. He did not simply want to replace those presently in power with others who were not yet in power. He was looking at something more radical than that. He took the values of his time, in all their variety, and turned them on their heads. He was busy with a *social* revolution, rather than a *political* one, a social revolution that called for a deep spiritual conversion....Jesus' sayings, especially those that were collected into the Sermon on the Mount, were subversive of almost everything his contemporaries took for granted.[1]

In the gospels, the "poor" are not only those with few or no possessions, and not only those whose poverty is "spiritual." In the biblical context the poor are the "little people" who are incapable of standing up for themselves and hence, by reason of their need and sorry state, are God's protected ones. The designation "poor" is not an idealization. The poor do really need help, the hungry stand in need of nourishment, the mourning are visibly sorrowing. All cry out for compassion. The "poor" to whom Jesus proclaimed the good news of the kingdom, and whom he pronounced "blessed," are not those whom he proposed as models of virtue but are persons literally "down and out." The kingdom of God, the consolation of the new age, is granted to the weak and despised—to those who suffer, who weep, who sorrow.

Following Luke's version of the beatitudes (6:20–23) are the "woes" of vv. 24–26, a construct of the evangelist. Yet, the warning, "Woe to you who are rich," is true to the stance of Jesus. The popular assumption was that wealth was a sign of God's blessing. Jesus proclaimed the opposite: It is not the rich who are blessed or fortunate, but the poor. This does not mean that destitution is a good thing, or that the poor will one day become rich. The poor are told that they should consider themselves fortunate; the rich are the unfortunate ones. They are the ones who will find it very difficult to adapt to the world of the kingdom where everything will be shared. The rich will find it very painful to share. The poor know how to share.[2]

Women

In the context of the culture of the day, the encounters of Jesus with women are remarkable. More significantly, they are always positive. A look at the more notable of them will make the point. This, of course, is not the whole picture; women do figure prominently below, under other headings.

In Mark 5:21–43 an encounter with a troubled woman gives a precious glimpse of the courtesy of Jesus. On his way to the home of Jairus he had sensed that a person of faith had invoked his healing power by touching his cloak.

He asked, "Who touched my clothes?" His blunt disciples looked at him, pityingly; he was thronged by a crowd and complained that someone had touched him! Jesus knew who that someone was: a woman, a woman, moreover, who suffered from a chronic hemorrhage and was therefore ritually unclean. She had no business being in a crowd and, by touching Jesus, rendered him ritually unclean also; or so others would have reckoned. While for her, the social consequences were not as grave as for the unfortunate leper (1:40–41), she was obliged to live in quiet isolation. Jesus had no patience with such restrictive purity regulations. Later (v. 41) he took the hand of a young woman (twelve years of age)—a gesture inappropriate for a religious leader. He was concerned with people, intent on liberation from physical and social suffering. Jesus did not scold the woman for her "reprehensible" conduct. Instead, he commended her faith. And he made a point, not only of speaking gently to her, but of addressing her respectfully as "daughter," that is, daughter of Abraham and Sarah, a child of God.

Luke (13:10–17) records a similar situation. At a sabbath synagogue session, Jesus healed a woman who had been crippled for eighteen years. The ruler of the synagogue regarded the healing as a breach of sabbath rest and petulantly complained to the people: "There are six days on which work ought to be done; come on those days and be cured, and not on the sabbath day" (v. 14). Jesus sharply criticized the narrow legalism that can frame laws for the welfare of animals and neglect a daughter of Abraham—one of the chosen people. That title of honor, "daughter of Abraham," is rarely attested. Jesus used it with refreshing naturalness.

Jesus Our Brother

In John 4:1–42 a weary Jesus sat by a well in hostile Samaria (v. 60)—a rare glimpse, in the Fourth Gospel, of his vulnerable humanity. "How is it that you, a Jew, ask of me, a woman of Samaria?" (v. 9), has a world of meaning crammed into a single question. Why this breach of convention that a man should so casually address a lone woman? And a Jew ought to know better than to ask a favor of a Samaritan! Later, the disciples could not hide their surprise at such conduct: "They were astonished that he was speaking with a woman" (v. 27). But the woman had spoken in reply to Jesus' request for a drink, and a dialogue was afoot. In a striking switch, Jesus moved from asking the woman for a drink of water to offering her a drink (v. 10). The subsequent dialogue falls outside our scope. Sufficient to observe that the declaration of the Samaritans to the woman, "it is no longer because of what you have said that we believe" (v. 42), does not imply imperfect faith on her part. Instead, "this woman is the first and only person (presented) in the life of Jesus through whose words of witness a group of people is brought to 'come and see' and 'to believe in Jesus.' "[3]

In Luke 8:2–3 the women (Mary, Joanna, Susanna, and "many others"), healed by Jesus, served him and his disciples out of their resources. *Diakonein* means "to serve," with the connotation of waiting on someone. It was the traditional service of slaves and women. Jesus transformed the meaning of the term: "Who is greater, the one who is at table or the one who serves? Is it not the one at the table? But I am among you as one who serves" (Luke 22:27). *Ho diakonon* (one who serves) is now an honorific designation. The antithetical roles of servant and ruler are paradoxically coupled. To serve (*diakonein*), a function proper to women, is applied to men who have a leadership role. It characterizes the manner in which leadership ought to be exercised. It is obvious that, along the lines of this model, women should readily qualify for leadership. For his part, Paul took it for granted that women worked in ministry on equal terms with men. For instance, in Philippians 4:3 he observes that the women Euodia and Syntyche had "struggled beside me in the work of the gospel, together with Clement and the rest of my co-workers." And there is the list of prominent women in Romans 16. Paul's example was, unhappily, not followed.

In the gospel narrative, women continue to be prominent in the passion story and after the resurrection. They are shown to be supportive of Jesus—it is their response to the kindness Jesus had shown to them. Mark's story of the anointing of Jesus (14:3–9) is located at Bethany (v. 11), in the house of "Simon the leper," doubtless one known in the circle where the story originated. The woman is not named; interest falls on the words of Jesus (vv. 7–9). She is, obviously, a disciple—how else might one account for her gesture? Her anointing was, implicitly, a royal anointing. Jesus graciously accepted anointing but related it to his death. This woman had made a lovely gesture, more meaningful than she knew. She, the woman disciple, showed an understanding that the men disciples lacked (see Matt 26:8). Her gracious deed will win her immortality: "Truly, I tell you, wherever the good news is proclaimed in the whole world, what she has done will be told in remembrance of her" (v. 9). The deed of this woman is firmly highlighted. But what has happened to the story in Christian tradition? Has that "lovely deed" become a prominent feature in the gospel knowledge of Christians? She has been left in her marginal anonymity.

Jesus Our Brother

The Twelve had fled at the arrest of Jesus (Mark 14:50). Yet, Jesus had not been wholly deserted—a little group of women disciples remained (14:40–44). Mark says of them: "They used to follow him and provided for him when he was in Galilee; and there were many other women who had come with him up to Jerusalem" (15:41). The women had "followed" him—*akoleuthein* is a technical term for discipleship. And they had "served" Jesus: they are authentic disciples. Although this is the only place in the gospel where the discipleship of women is mentioned in explicit terms, we should not overlook the reference to "many other women." It is because they had continued to follow him, if only "at a distance" (v. 40)—as women they could not be at the very place of execution—that the final message was entrusted to them.

In Matt 28:1–15 the women came to "see" the tomb (and not to anoint the body of Jesus as in Mark 16:1–8). In Matthew that office is ruled out because of the guard at the tomb. The interpreting angel addressed his glad tidings to the women: they must not fear but should rejoice because the crucified Jesus they sought is now the Risen One. With joy they run to tell the other disciples. Suddenly, Jesus met them. Here, uniquely, in stories of encounter with the risen Jesus, he was recognized at once. His message is that they must hasten to announce the good news: they will meet Jesus again in Galilee. Go and tell "my brothers," those who had failed him so miserably. It is the graciousness of total forgiveness. The word of God is for all ages; there is surely a message for our day in this passage. *Women* were the first to hear the good news of the resurrection; *women* were the first heralds of the resurrection (vv. 7, 10). *Women* were the first to meet the risen Lord—rather, to be met by him! When will the church hearken to this word?

In 20:11–18 John has reduced the "women" of the synoptics to Mary Magdalene. Mary addressed a "stranger." She recognized him at his calling her by name. This is reminiscent of John 10:3—the Good Shepherd "calls his own sheep by name." Her joyous instinct was to cling to him. She has to learn that the time for association with the earthly Jesus is past. His "hour" was still in process—the "hour" of death, resurrection, and return to the Father. Mary was given a mission: apostle to the disciples. She carried an astounding message. Up to now, in the narrative, Jesus alone was Son. Now he spoke of my Father and *your* Father, my God and *your* God! The God and Father of Jesus is God and Father of his "brethren." Christians are no longer Jesus' disciples, nor even his "friends" (15:15), but his brothers and sisters. This astounding truth was first confided to a woman.

Children

If Jesus' attitude toward women was unconventional, no less so was his regard for children. The passage Mark 10:13–16 is a pronouncement story showing Jesus' attitude toward children. Mark has delightfully brought the little scene to life: mothers eager to present their little ones to Jesus; the disciples officiously "protecting" Jesus and demanding, "Get those brats out of here!"; Jesus' indignation at their rebuff to children; his taking them into his arms. The point of the narrative lies in the sayings. The disposition of a child—receptivity, a willingness to accept what is freely given—is necessary for all who would enter the kingdom. Children, better than any other, are suited for the kingdom, since the kingdom is a gift that must be welcomed with simplicity.

In Mark 9:35–37 Jesus read a lesson to his disciples. He took a little child from the arms of its mother. "Taking it in his arms" (v. 36) is proper to Mark (see 10:16), a vivid touch in his style. In that culture, no self-respecting man would have done the same. This little gesture spoke volumes of Jesus' reverence for people—especially the most helpless of all.

Sinners

The parables of Luke 15 that deal with the reprieve of sinners are Jesus' answer to the "scandal" of the Pharisees: "All the tax-collectors and sinners were coming to listen to him. And the Pharisees and scribes were grumbling and saying, 'This fellow welcomes sinners and eats with them'" (15:1–2). When we add two sayings of Jesus, "Those who are well have no need of a physician, but those who are sick; I have come to call not the righteous but sinners" (Mark 2:17); "The Son of Man came to seek out and to save the lost" (Luke 2:17), and instance the generous response of a forgiven sinner (Luke 7:36–50), we get a thorough view of Jesus' regard for sinners. The parables and sayings are a vindication of the good news for three reasons: because in them sinners are said to be sick people (only the sick need a doctor) and grateful people (only those burdened with debt know the relief of remission); because they reveal the nature of God as loving merciful Parent; because they show sinners as, in some way, closer to God than the "righteous."

These parables show God's compassion for sinners, not as a timeless general truth, but as realized in the ministry of Jesus. The lost sheep is dearer to the Shepherd, this Jesus, precisely because it is lost! The parables demonstrate that the words and deeds of Jesus are inseparable. He is not a teacher of morals outlining principles of conduct. Instead, his attitude toward and daily life with the poor are the models of our behavior. He has fulfilled perfectly—as he no doubt inspired—the words of counsel offered later to his disciples: "Little children, let us love, not in word or speech, but in truth and in action" (1 John 3:18).

Jesus' regard for, and his concern for, people will emerge clearly in the consideration, below, of his distinctive traits and characteristics.

Table Fellowship

The story of Jesus feeding the multitude, attested in all four gospels, has association with a meal pattern throughout the ministry. Matthew (11:18–19) sets up a contrast between the Baptist and Jesus: "John came neither eating nor drinking...the Son of Man came eating and drinking, and they say, 'Look, a glutton and a drunkard, a friend of tax collectors and sinners!'" The saying presupposes a well-established reputation. Jesus, unlike the Baptist, was no ascetic. This squares with Jesus' contention that, as long as he was with them, the disciples cannot fast (Mark 2:19).

Jesus showed his concern for the socially despised and for "sinners" (nonobservant Jews) precisely through table fellowship with them. They had been stripped of hope by the "righteous," who despised and avoided them. Now this manifest man of God went out of his way to break bread with them, to seek communion with them. He was assuring them that, unlike the righteous, God did not regard them as outcasts. Doubtless, he hoped that they would change their ways; but he did not threaten. And he did not demand that they perform what the law stipulated if they were to be reckoned as righteous. One thinks, for instance, of Zacchaeus in his sycamore tree. A preacher of repentance would have wagged his finger and read Zacchaeus—a spectacularly captive hearer—the riot act. Instead, Jesus casually invited himself to dinner in his home. Zacchaeus must nearly have toppled from his perch in surprised delight. A sermon would have left him unaffected—he had been too often preached at. The novel approach changed his life (Luke 19:1–10). Jesus' concern reached out to all. He welcomed invitations to dine with Pharisees (see Luke 7:36; 14:1).

We may find the key to Jesus' understanding of his practice of table fellowship with outcasts in Matthew 8:11: "I tell you, many will come from east and west and will eat with Abraham and Isaac and Jacob in the kingdom of heaven" (see Luke 13:28). His shared meals were a preparation for, and anticipation of, the great banquet in the kingdom. Hence, his pronouncement at the Last Supper: "Truly I tell you, I will never again drink of the fruit of the vine until that day when I drink it new in the kingdom of God " (Mark 14:25). Moreover, in table fellowship with sinners, Jesus was displaying the Father's preferential option for sinners (see Luke 15:7, 10). If, then, at the Last Supper, Jesus asserted that his next drink of wine would be at table in the fullness of the kingdom, he implied that the supper was the climax of a series of meals that celebrated, in anticipation, the joy of the banquet. They were meals that, indeed, opened the banquet to all who would not deliberately reject the invitation.

3

JESUS OF NAZARETH: TRAITS

THIS SECTION DEALS WITH traits or characteristics of Jesus. The treatment is of unequal length, depending on the prominence of a particular trait in the gospels and/or its importance in an overall picture of the humanity of Jesus.

Faith

Because the Hebrew Bible does not really have a word for "faith," what we have come to term *faith* is, in the Old Testament, described rather than defined. The description mainly concerns the relationship of Israel to the Lord and the relationship to the Lord of some key figures of Israel, notably Abraham and Moses. In either case—group or individual—the ground of faith is trust in the faithfulness of God. At its most basic, faith is the attitude that discerns God creatively in action in the world and in human life. This discernment prompts the commitment of oneself in trust and obedience. The faithfulness of God assures God's fulfillment of the obligations assumed in creating humankind and, particularly, in his calling of Abraham and choice of Israel to be his people. "Faith" is, simply, trust in the faithfulness of God.

The New Testament has a term for faith: *pistis*. It reflects its Old Testament background and means much more than "belief" or intellectual assent. It means thoroughgoing commitment. It is the complete response, in total freedom, of a human to God in a spirit of trust, obedience, and endurance. Faith is letting God be God in one's life. This was surely true of Jesus of Nazareth. He was, supremely, a man of faith. Increasingly, New Testament scholars acknowledge that, in Galatians and Romans, Paul understands *pistis Iésou Christou* (e.g., Gal 2:16, 20; 3:22; Rom 3:22, 26) as "the faith *of* Jesus Christ"—his total trust in the Father and his own consequent faithfulness. Jesus lived his life in faith so understood: "My food is to do the will of him who sent me and to complete his work" (John 4:34).

Jesus' faith, his total obedience of the Father, is well documented. Faith *and* hope—for hope is the other side of faith. This faith/hope is present in the "after three days rise again" at the conclusion of each passion prediction (Mark 8:31; 9:31; 10:34). Before the raising of Lazarus he prayed: "Father, I thank you for having heard me. I know that you always hear me" (John 11:41–42). His prayer at Gethsemane—"Not what I want, but what you want" (Mark 14:35–36)—strikingly articulates his faithful obedience. At the Last Supper he spoke with assurance of drinking wine in the kingdom of God (Mark 14:25). He could bluntly inform the high priest: "You will see the Son of Man seated at the right hand of the Power" (Mark 14:62). He knew when his "hour" had come and prayed to the Father to "glorify" him so that the Father might be "glorified"—revealed as the God of infinite mercy. The impending death of Jesus will reveal, once for all, the all-embracing, saving love of Father and Son (John 17:1–5; see 3:16–17; Rom 8:31–39). A dying Jesus could confidently promise the "good thief," "Truly I tell you, today you will be with me in Paradise" (Luke 23:43). And Luke gives, as the last words of Jesus, a prayer of utter serenity: "Father, into your hands I commit my spirit" (23:46). He was, first and last, the faithful one, *ho martys ho pistos*, the faithful witness (Rev 1:5). He was the faithful one "with whom the Father was well pleased" (Mark 1:11; 9:7). His faith, his trust in the faithful Father, would be tested.

Testing

> We do not have a high priest who is unable to sympathize with our weaknesses, but we have one who in every respect has been tested as we are, yet without sin (Heb 4:15).

> Because he himself was tested by what he suffered, he is able to help those who are being tested (Heb 2:18).

Jesus, baptized by John, began his mission as disciple of the Baptist. He went on to launch his own distinctive mission. This was a major decision that involved other decisions. He was thoroughly convinced of his calling. He had, however, to work out for himself how his mission would be carried through; he had to learn how, perfectly, to represent his Abba. To make the Abba known: that was his role. The temptation stories, placed, dramatically, by Matthew and Luke, before the opening of his mission, incorporate decisions he was to arrive at throughout his mission.

The Letter to the Hebrews tells us that Jesus was "one who in every respect has been tested as we are, yet without sin" (4:15). How are we to understand that "without sin"? Is it *non posse peccare* or *posse non peccare*? That is: incapable of sin or able not to sin? In the past, the preference was for the former: Jesus was wholly incapable of sin.

But that makes testing or temptation pointless. The author of Hebrews is quite sure that the testing was real. What was involved is brought out, splendidly, by C. H. Dodd in his commentary on Romans 6:9–10: "death no longer has dominion over him (Christ); the death he died, he died to sin once for all."

> The sense of these words must be understood from other passages in which Paul speaks of the life and death of Jesus in relation to the condition of the world. Mankind was bound in the servitude of Sin, established in the "flesh." Thus the natural, flesh-and-blood life of man was the territory, so to speak, of Sin, and all dwellers on that territory Sin claimed as his own. Christ, by his incarnation, became a denizen of "the flesh." Sin put in its claim. In other words, Jesus was tempted to sin, as we all are tempted, in such forms as sin might take for one in his situation. But instead of yielding, and acknowledging Sin's dominion, as we all do, he rendered a perfect obedience to God "and became obedient to the point of death" (Phil 2:8). Jesus, in plain terms, died rather than sin; and so his death instead of being a sign of the victory of Sin over man's true nature, was a sign of the complete rout of Sin in a decisive engagement.[1]

THE WILDERNESS

Each gospel shows Jesus subjected to temptation, to testing. Even John, who does not mention the forty days in the wilderness, shows moments in the mission when Jesus' fidelity came under pressure. The Letter to the Hebrews, we have seen, is emphatic about Jesus being tested. Matthew and Luke (Matt 4:1–11; Luke 4:1–13) believed that Jesus was really tested; otherwise, their temptation story is meaningless. They have expressed, in stylized form, the broadly based New Testament conviction that Jesus had to struggle to remain faithful to God's will.

At the start of the passage 4:1–11 Matthew shows Jesus experiencing what Israel had experienced in the desert—with the radical difference that the Son will conquer where God's son Israel had failed (Deut 8:2–5). The tempter immediately latches on to the question of Jesus' sonship. (It ought to be obvious that a literalist interpretation—and, a fortiori, presentation—of the "temptations" must be avoided. This is a sophisticated piece of writing and one must correctly grasp Matthew's intent). At the baptism Jesus had been solemnly acclaimed as God's Son (3:17); the question now is: how will he *function* as God's Son? Jesus will not abuse his sonship to his own advantage (first temptation). In quoting Deuteronomy 8:3 Jesus had urged his trust in God; now he is challenged to turn that trust into crass presumption (second temptation). Building on the promise that the Messiah-Son would have the nations for his inheritance (Ps 3:6–8), the "ruler of this world" (John 12:31; 16:11) presents himself as a god to be worshipped—only to be unceremoniously repudiated (third temptation). This bizarre episode is readily understandable when we consider the basic temptation of Israel to idolatry and when we observe that Jesus' reply is an emphatic assertion of God's fundamental command to Israel: monotheism (Deut 6:13).

In each of the three ripostes to "the devil" Jesus cited texts from Deuteronomy, and these texts are the key to the meaning of each scene.

1. "One does not live by bread alone" (Deut 8:3). Jesus had been challenged to provide food miraculously for himself, to use his authority as Son apart from the Father's design.
2. "Do not put the Lord your God to the test" (6:16). Again, Jesus was challenged to use his power on his own behalf, this time to dazzle his contemporaries and conform to their image of a heaven-sent messiah.
3. "Worship the Lord your God and serve only him" (6:13). Jesus was challenged to be wholly autonomous, to do things entirely his way. His firm decision is that, if he has to have *exousia*, authority, he will have it from the Father alone. He will learn that his exercise of authority will ever be as *diakonia*, service.

The three scenes serve to illustrate the sort of decisions Jesus had to make in fulfilling his mission as Son. A consistent biblical pattern, representing God's respect for humankind, is the role of mediator in God's dealing with people. Jesus was mediator (Heb 5:1–3; 8:6). In keeping with the reality of the human situation, God saw it fitting that the Son who leads men and women to salvation should be made perfect through suffering (2:10). Jesus learned from his suffering what obedience to God's will asked of humankind—"and having been made perfect he became the source of eternal salvation for all who obey him" (5:9).

GETHSEMANE (MARK 14:32–43)

Mark's Gethsemane scene is a poignant moment of decision. It shows that Jesus did not fully understand God's way; it shows that he did not want to die: "Abba,

Father, for you all things are possible, remove this cup from me; yet, not what I want, but what you want" (v. 36). While we may plausibly assert that *Abba* was Jesus' preferred address to his God, the word *abba* appears only once in the gospels—here in Mark 14:36. Its presence here is fitting: The familiar title seems to be wrested from Jesus at this awful moment. He explicitly prayed that the cup be taken from him. He did not contemplate suffering and a horrible death with stoical calm. He was appalled at the prospect. He knew fear. He was brave as he arose above his fear to embrace what his God asked. But he must know if the path that opened before him was indeed the way that God would have him walk. He found assurance in prayer: the utterance of his trustful "Abba" already included "thy will be done." His prayer did not go unanswered—though the answer was paradoxical. As the Letter to the Hebrews puts it: "he was heard because of his reverent submission" (5:7). The obedient Son cried out to the Father and put himself wholly in the hands of the Father. It is a thoroughly human moment. God *seemed* to be asking this way of Jesus. Was God *really* asking what he seemed to ask? Jesus found the answer in prayer. There will be moments in our lives when we, also, must question: Is God really asking of me what he seems to ask? Jesus has shown where the answer is to be found.

If Jesus said of the disciples, "the spirit indeed is willing, but the flesh is weak" (Mark 14:38), that statement is not irrelevant to his own situation. Jesus himself had experienced human vulnerability: distress, agitation, and grief even to the point of death, to the point of asking the Father that the hour might pass him by and cup be taken away. "Hour" and "cup" indicate the historical moment and the imminent prospect of appalling death. But this, too, was the eschatological hour of the final struggle, the great *peirasmos*, "trial," before the triumph of God's kingdom. "The Son of Man is given over to the hands of sinners" (14:41). In the Old Testament God gives over the wicked to punishment; here, in contrast, a just man is "given over" by God. At the end Jesus invited his disciples: "Get up, let us be going!" (v. 42). Jesus still includes his disciples, even though they had failed him.[2]

Love

"Which commandment is the first of all?" (Mark 12:28). This question of a scribe to Jesus was one the rabbis sought to answer. They looked for a commandment that outweighed all the others, one that might be regarded as the basic principle on which the whole law was grounded. Jesus had been asked to name a commandment; he responded by naming two commandments: " 'You shall love the Lord your God with all your heart, and with all your soul, and with all your strength.' The second is this, 'You shall love your neighbor as yourself.' There is no other commandment greater than these" (vv. 30–31). This reply is of great importance. It would seem that Jesus was the first to bring together these two commands of love of God and love of neighbor (see Deut 6:4; Lev 19:18). Love of neighbor arises out of love of God. He had taken and welded the two precepts into one.

In the synoptic gospels only here and in the parallel passages Matthew 22:37 and Luke 11:42 is there word on human love of God. It appears sparingly in the rest of the New Testament. The emphasis is, rather, on God's love of humankind. And this is as it should be. It is because God has first loved us that we love God (Rom 5:5, 8; 1 John

4:11). And there is the test of the authenticity of our love of God: "Those who do not love a brother or sister whom they have seen, cannot love God whom they have not seen. The commandment we have from him [Jesus] is this: those who love God must love their brothers and sisters also" (1 John 4:20–21). Jesus had shown in his life and death the quality of his twofold love. His love for God motivated his total dedication to his mission. His love for humankind marked him as one who had come to serve the saving purpose of God, one who had laid down his life as a ransom for humankind (Mark 10:45; see John 15:13).

The scribe's reply (12:32–33) is proper to Mark: "You are right, Teacher; you have truly said that 'he is one, and besides him there is no other'; and 'to love him with all the heart, and with all the understanding, and with all the strength,' and 'to love one's neighbor as oneself'—this is much more important than all whole burnt offerings and sacrifices." He agrees fully with Jesus' answer and further specifies that the loving service of others is more important than elaborate cult. His insistence on love with the whole heart is a recognition that love cannot be measured. Love is incompatible with legalism that sets limits, that specifies what we should do and should avoid. Jesus' assurance that the scribe is not far from the kingdom of God (12:34) is, in truth, an invitation.

Jesus was motivated by love: love of God and of humanity. Jesus' love of the Father is manifest, as is assurance that the Father loved him: "The Father loves the Son and shows him all that he himself is doing" (John 5:20)—because love is generous. Jesus shared this love: "As the Father has loved me so I have loved you" (John 15:9). His love was not for his disciples only, but for all: "I, when I am lifted up from the earth, will draw all to myself" (12:32).

While all of this is so, it is relevant and comforting to note instances of Jesus' love of individuals and of friends.

Perhaps the saddest story in the gospel is that of Mark 10:17–22, the failure of one whom Jesus loved to answer his call. Entry into the kingdom is the matter and issue as Jesus was asked what one must do to inherit eternal life. He began to answer by pointing to the duties toward one's neighbor prescribed in the Decalogue; but he knew that observance of the law could not be the whole answer. He was drawn to the man—"Jesus, looking at him, loved him"—and invited him to become his disciple. This aspiring follower had to learn that discipleship is costly: he, a wealthy man, was asked to surrender the former basis of his security and find security in Jesus' word. He failed to recognize that following Jesus was the true treasure, the one pearl of great price (Matt 13:44, 46) beyond all his possessions.

Luke and John inform us of a quite special relationship between Jesus and the family of Martha, Mary, and Lazarus in Bethany, and his friendship was warmest with the women. As a sexually mature man, he had an easy rapport with women, whom he treated with unfailing courtesy. On his final journey to Jerusalem, "Jesus entered a certain village" (Luke 10:38); from John 11:1 we learn that it was Bethany. The familiar relationship between Jesus and the women (Luke does not mention Lazarus), explicitly remarked in John 11:5—"Jesus loved Martha and her sister"—is, in Luke 10:38–42, graphically portrayed. An exasperated Martha does not hesitate to point out that it is Jesus' fault that she had been left on her own in preparation of a meal for Jesus and his disciples (v. 40). He gently chides her for her agitation (v. 41). There is textual confusion with regard to v. 42a. The longer reading, impressively attested ("few things are necessary or only one"), refers to the needless concern of Martha—one dish will suffice. The shorter reading ("there is need of only one thing") may well be authentic: Martha is told that the one thing necessary is the presence of the Lord and the word that he imparts. He, indeed, is host rather than guest. Mary, drinking in his words (v. 39), is displaying "undivided devotion to the Lord" (1 Cor 7:35). Here the role of Martha is contrasted with that of Mary: a disciple sitting at the feet of Jesus and listening to his word (Luke 10:39a). A notable feature is this depiction of a woman as student of the word and the Lord's emphatic approval of the role.

In John 11:1–53 we learn that the sisters sent word to Jesus that their brother Lazarus was gravely ill: "Lord, he whom you love is ill" (v. 3). On his delayed arrival at Bethany Jesus found that Lazarus had been buried for four days (v. 17). When she had been informed that he had arrived in the village, Martha came to meet him; Mary stayed at home. The sisters display the same temperaments as in Luke 10:38–41. Martha's gentle rebuke of Jesus— "Lord, if you had been here, my brother would not have died" (v. 21) is later repeated by her sister (v. 32). Jesus shared Mary's grief: "Jesus began to weep" (v. 35). The bystanders commented: "See how he loved him!" (v. 36). Sandra Schneiders observes: "Jesus' tears are an honest sharing in Mary's grief and perhaps her anger at death, the enemy of all life. Jesus, in his most fully human moment in the Fourth Gospel, legitimates human agony in the face of death, an agony he will feel for himself as he shrinks from the passion in chapter 12....Death is real and so is the suffering it causes. Faith is not compatible with despair, but it is no stranger to tears."[3]

Six days before the fateful Passover, Jesus left his wilderness retreat (John 10:40–42) and came again to his friends at Bethany (12:1–8). Martha, practical hostess, served a meal. The contrast between the women persists. Mary, the romantic one, took a flask of expensive ointment and anointed Jesus' feet, wiping them off with her long hair. The perfume filled the house—the perfume of Mary's love.

Prayer

"Descended from David according to the flesh" (Rom 1:3), Jesus was a son of Israel. As an observant Jew he was, by definition, a man of prayer. Aside from Luke, who had a special interest in prayer, the evangelists do not elaborate on Jesus' prayer life. This is not surprising. Simply, they, like him, took prayer for granted. We, Christians of another culture and of the twenty-first century, cannot be so casual. We demand reasons for everything and we ask why we ought to pray in the first place. The realization that Jesus was a man of prayer may give us food for thought. It is also a factor that underlines his humanity.

There is no doubt at all that Jesus did pray. Mark, with attractive candor, tells us that Jesus' addiction to prayer was something of a trial to his disciples. The evangelist has sketched a sample day in the early Galilean mission, at Capernaum (Mark 1:21–34), a day of enthusiastic reception and of great promise. His disciples, caught up in the excitement, were chagrined when Jesus went missing (v. 37)—"In the morning, while it was still very dark, he got up and went out to a deserted place, and there he prayed" (1:35). Typically, Mark has said so much in few words. Jesus had slept (he "got up"), had snatched a few hours of sleep. For his mission he needed deeper refreshment, a more potent source of energy, and he found it in prayer to his Abba. His Father was the Sustainer of all. As one "like us in every respect" (Heb 2:17), Jesus was wholly dependent on his God. He turned, spontaneously, to an Abba who would support him, who would back him in his endeavors. Though one sent, he had to plow his own furrow. But he was not alone because the Father was with him. The prayer of Jesus, his whole prayerful trust in his Abba, is an essential ingredient of any meaningful Christology.

Prayer of and by Jesus, by example, not by contrived design, is meant to alert the disciple to his or her dependence on God. If the Son found a need and a joy in converse with his Father, he could expect that the other children of God, his sisters and brothers, would, too, experience that need and that happiness. The comforting fact is that Jesus, now as our High Priest, has not ended his prayer. Returned to the Father he has no need any more to pray for himself. Henceforth he is the high priest who prays *for us*, who makes intercession for us without respite (see Heb 7:25).

It ought not to surprise us that prayer of Jesus should figure in the Gospel of Luke. The third evangelist, with his notable interest in prayer, could not have overlooked the prayer of the Lord. It is he who tells us that Jesus prayed at the baptism: "Now when all the people were baptized, and when Jesus had been baptized and was praying, the heaven was opened, and the Holy Spirit descended upon him in bodily form like a dove. And a voice came from heaven, 'You are my Son, the Beloved; with you I am well pleased'" (Luke 3:21–22). Luke, indeed, gives the impression that it was as response to the prayer of Jesus that the Holy Spirit came upon him. And not impression only; it is Luke's intent that we should see it so. Later (11:13), we learn that the heavenly Father grants the Holy Spirit to

51

those who ask. Jesus' prayer was a plea to the Father—not unlike the prayer of Job, though apart here from the context of darkness—that God would manifest himself, would declare their relationship.

A phrase in Luke is revealing when we compare parallel gospel passages. Mark and Matthew agree that Jesus, on coming to his "hometown" (which Luke names as Nazareth) on a sabbath, began to teach (Mark 6:1–2; Matt 13:54). Luke made a further point: "Jesus went to the synagogue on the sabbath day, as was his custom" (Luke 4:16)—Jesus is characterized as a "regular churchgoer"! Luke does not have it all his own way. One might even say that, because of Luke's avowed interest in prayer, reference to the prayer of Jesus by the other evangelists has added weight. At least, it assures us that Luke had latched on to a firm datum of the tradition.

According to the authors of the three synoptic gospels, Jesus prayed at Gethsemane, he prayed after the multiplication of loaves, he prayed in Capernaum after he had healed many. Luke tells of the prayer of Jesus in eight further circumstances. He prayed at the baptism (Luke 3:21), he slipped away to a lonely place to pray (5:16), and, before selecting the Twelve, he spent the whole night in prayer (6:12). He prayed before Peter's confession of him as Messiah (9:18); later he would tell Peter that he had prayed especially for him (22:32). He prayed at the transfiguration (9:28–29) and it was the sight of him at prayer that moved his disciples to ask him to teach them to pray (11:1). He prayed on the cross for all who had engineered his death (22:34). The surrender of his life to the Father was a prayer (23:46).

Jesus had often recommended prayer to his disciples: persevering prayer like that of the importunate friend (11:5–13) or of the widow faced with an unjust judge (18:1–8).

They must pray to receive the Spirit (11:13). In short, they ought to pray at all times (21:36). But their prayer should be real prayer, like that of the tax collector (18:13).

In the Fourth Gospel the farewell discourse (chaps. 13–16) closes with a prayer in chapter 17. This prayer is, in its manner, a commentary on the passion of Jesus which reflects the drift of the fourth evangelist's emphasis: the coming of Jesus, revealer of the Father into this world (John 17:1–12), then the return of Jesus to the Father. Structurally, the prayer falls into three parts as Jesus prays for himself (vv. 1–5), for his disciples (vv. 6–19), and for the community of the future who "believe through their word" (vv. 20–26).

The third petition reaches to us. Jesus will make the Father more fully known. But that will be at the cost of love. It is only as a loving community that the love of Father and Son can be experienced, that Father and Son can be truly known. Only in loving one another can the disciples be one with Jesus; only so will he dwell among them and be in them. It is the earnest prayer of Jesus that this be so: "I pray for him" (17:20).

Conviction of the companionship of God was the secret of Jesus' own prayer life. What moved him to rise a long while before dawn and go out to pray in a lonely place so that he was long absent from his disciples (see Mark 1:35)? Or what made him "go out to the mountain to pray, and to spend the night in prayer to God" (Luke 6:12)? In short, what was it that moved him to mark his prayer with a new, intimate mode of address: Abba? It was his abiding sense of companionship with the Father, his knowing he was never alone. That which Jesus felt with his Father was the same companionship his disciples, with all Christians, came to feel with him. "Remember, I am with you always, to the end of the age" (Matt 28:20).

53

Religion

Jesus was an observant Jew who wholly respected the authentic religious tradition of his people. He observed the sabbath; he was a regular attendant at sabbath synagogue worship. He respected the traditional practices of almsgiving, prayer, and fasting (Matt 6:1–18). He went on pilgrimage to Jerusalem for the great feasts: Passover, Tabernacles, Dedication (John 2:13; 7:10, 14; 10:22). He revered the temple as the house of God (Mark 11:17; John 2:16). All the while, however, he was very critical of the manner in which, and to the extent that, "traditions" had overwhelmed religious practice. His own free attitude toward religion brought him into conflict with those for whom religion meant meticulous observance of rules and regulations. Jesus emerges both as upholder and as a radical critic of religion. To be positively critical of any religious system is surely an attribute of maturity.

It is clear from the gospels that Jesus had *exousia*—authority—from God. It is equally clear that this power of his had no shade of domination. The gospels indeed show Jesus having facile authority over evil spirits (the exorcisms) and over nature (the stilling of the storm). But Jesus' authority did not extend to lording it over people. In relation to people, he was largely helpless. The hallmark of his use of authority in relation to people was consistently and emphatically that of *diakonia*, service. If Jesus served others, it was always from a position of strength. He would not do what others wanted him to do unless it be consonant with God's will. He would lead, but he would not control.

Jesus certainly confronted the religious authorities, but without seeking to impose his authority on them. He was content to hold the mirror up to them, urging them to discern in their attitude and conduct a betrayal of God's rule. But that was the measure of it. Response was their responsibility. Jesus sought no advantage from his authority. He laid claim to no titles—it was up to others to identify him. He was, after all, the one who had come "to serve, and to give his life as a ransom for many" (Mark 10:45). In short, Jesus, in his authority, as in all else, mirrored God. For God, the God of infinite power, is never a God of force. The Son never would, nor ever did, resort to force.

SABBATH

Sabbath observance is specified, in well-nigh identical terms, in both versions of the "Ten Words" or commandments: "Remember the sabbath day and keep it holy" (Exod 20:8; Deut. 5:12). Apart from declaring it to be a day free of work, the Torah does not further specify how the sabbath is to be "kept holy." During the Babylonian Exile and especially in the Second Temple era, an elaborate system of sabbath observance evolved. This formed a major feature of "the tradition of the elders," which Jesus essentially rejected (see Mark 7:1–13). Relevant here is the motive for sabbath observance proposed in Deuteronomy. While in Exodus the sabbath is linked to God's sabbath rest (Exod 20:11), Deuteronomy links it to deliverance from Egyptian slavery: "Remember that you were a slave in the land of Egypt, and the Lord your God brought you out from there with a mighty hand and an outstretched arm; therefore the Lord your God commanded you to keep the sabbath day" (Deut 5:15). In Jesus' view this celebration of freedom had become a new slavery. It made no sense.

The frequent reference in the gospels to critique of Jesus' alleged violation of sabbath observance underlines his consistent attitude. He sought to set the sabbath free. That it needed to be set free is illustrated in the episode of Mark 3:1–6: an act of healing is regarded as a breach of sabbath observance. Note the querulous synagogue leader of Luke 13:14 in reaction to Jesus' healing of a crippled woman on the sabbath: "There are six days in which work ought to be done; come on those days to be cured, and not on the sabbath day." Jesus' assessment of sabbath observance is stated with emphatic clarity in the conflict story of Mark 2:23–28: "The sabbath was made for humankind, and not humankind for the sabbath" (v. 27). Indeed, the declaration is of wider import. Decoded, it reads: Religion is to serve men and women; men and women are not to be enslaved by religion. He had defined the true meaning of religion—it is *for* men and women.

RITUAL OBSERVANCE

As the text of Mark 7:1–23 stands, a precise incident lay behind Jesus' dispute with the Pharisees and scribes. They had observed that the disciples of Jesus did not practice the ritual washing of hands before meals. In their eyes this constituted a transgression of the "tradition of the elders"—the *halakah,* or oral law. Those Pharisaic traditions claimed to interpret and complete the Mosaic Law and were regarded as equally authoritative and binding as the Mosaic prescriptions. Later rabbis would claim that the "ancestral law" constituted a second, oral law given, with the written law, to Moses on Sinai.

In responding to the charge of neglecting one observance (Mark 7:5), Jesus turned the debate on to a wider issue: the relative worth of Mosaic Law and oral law. He cited Isaiah 29:13 against the Pharisees, drawing a parallel between "human precepts" of which Isaiah spoke and the "human tradition" on which the Pharisees counted. Jesus rejected the oral law because it was the work of men (not the word of God) and because it could and did conflict with the law of God. The oral law had put casuistry above love. He instanced (vv. 9–13) a glaring example of casuistry run wild: a precise vow of dedication. A man might declare *korban*—that is, dedicated to God—the property or capital which, by right, should go to the support of his parents. Property thus made over by vow took on a sacred character; the parents had no more claim on it. In fact, such a vow was a legal fiction, a way of avoiding filial responsibility. But it was a vow and, as such, in rabbinical eyes, was binding and could not be dispensed. In this manner, a solemn duty enjoined by Torah (Exod 20:12) was set aside. Jesus could multiply examples, he declared (Mark 7:13). He was aware that one whose mind runs to casuistry loses all sense of proportion. Minute detail becomes more and more important. Law and observance become an obsession. People are defined in terms of conformity or of "sinful" departure from it. Casuists are regularly in positions of authority and make life miserable for others—especially the vulnerable. Jesus' concern was, first and always, people and their needs. Everything else was relative to that.

The criterion of clean and unclean (a strictly ritual principle) was at the root of Jewish concern with ritual purity. A saying of Jesus struck at the very distinction of clean and unclean, of sacred and secular: "There is nothing outside a person that by going in can defile, but the things that come out are what defile" (v. 15). At one stroke Jesus had set aside the whole concept of ritual impurity. Holiness does not lie in the realm of "clean" over against "unclean." It is not in the realm of things but in the realm of conduct. It is to be found in the human heart and is a matter of human responsibility. Mark's parenthetical comment—"Thus he declared all foods clean" (v. 19)—correctly caught the nuance of the saying. More generally, it is a flat denial that any external things or circumstances can separate one from God (see Rom 8:38–39). We can be separated from God only through our own attitude and behavior. Jesus' contrast between word of God and human law and his emphatic assertion of the priority of the former are, obviously, of abiding validity and moment. Religion has not always seen it so.

The gospel presentation of the scribes paints them, in our terms, as theologians and canon lawyers. They prided themselves on their meticulous religious observance. On both scores they (or some among them) invited and received deference; to that end they affected distinctive dress (see Matt 23:1–7). They claimed the "best seats" in the synagogue: directly in front of the ark containing the sacred scrolls and facing the people. The charge of v. 40 is more serious: "They devour widows' houses and for the sake of appearance say long prayers." In other words, they are accused of exploiting the social and financial vulnerability of widows.

The vignette of the "widow's mite" (vv. 41–44) may have found its setting here partly because of the word *widow* (vv. 40, 42). More to the point, Jesus' previous castigation of scribes as those who "devour widows' houses" is surely in mind. The "copper coin" (*lepton*) was the smallest in circulation. Mention of two coins is important: the woman might have kept one for herself. Instead, she threw both, "all she had to live on" into the treasury. This poor widow was a victim of religious establishment. She had been convinced that it was a "holy" thing to give her all to the temple. She is a tragic example of a situation Jesus had in mind when he declared: "Religion is for men and women, not men and women for religion" (see Mark 2:27).

The traditional understanding of the passage is very different. The widow is representative of genuine Jewish piety in contrast to the counterfeit piety of the scribes (or, of scribes characterized in vv. 38–39). Wealthy people had been generous (v. 41). This poor widow's mite was an immeasurably greater gift than theirs, for she had given her all—her "whole living" (v. 44). She had let go of every shred of security and had committed herself wholly to God., Indeed, Mark seems to take it in this sense. However, a nagging question remains. Jesus appears to commend a practically penniless widow for donating to a wealthy temple all she had to sustain her life. Indeed, he implicitly presents her as a model. She would give everything she had—and starve! Is this compatible with Jesus' distinctive concern for the poor and marginalized? I think not.

GOOD WORKS

Almsgiving, prayer, and fasting were traditional Jewish practices, admirable when performed simply, by sincere people. Jesus thoroughly approved of them. "Hypocrites" can make a holy show of these good ways. Jesus did not approve of public display of what was meant to be private practice (Matt 6:1–18). Moreover, despite his approval of the practice, he and his disciples did not fast. This was noted: "Why do John's disciples and the disciples of the Pharisees fast, but your disciples do not fast?" (Mark 2:18). By this Jesus distinguished himself and his disciples from all other Jews, thereby making a remarkable claim for his own person and mission.

Oaths and vows figured in Jewish religious practice. Jesus did not set much store by them. They could become a fertile field for casuistry. Some would maintain that to swear by the Temple's gold is binding—not an oath by the Temple! To swear by the gift on the altar is binding—not an oath by the altar (Matt 23:16–22)! Indeed, Jesus can declare: "Do not swear at all." The word of his disciples ought to be "Yes, Yes" or "No, No" (5:33–37). There should be no need of the formality of oath in their dealings with one another. One might ask how one may reconcile this absolute prohibition with later church practice—such as the intrusive obligation of the anti-Modernistic oath, and today, the demand of a modified oath. In tithing, the fatal flaw is of casuistry. You tithe the most insignificant of garden herbs and ignore the real matters of the law: justice, mercy, faith (see Matt 23:23–24). In the parable of the Pharisee and the tax-collector, the Pharisee, far beyond the demands of the law, paid tithe on all his possessions (Luke 18:12).

Jesus was critical of what might be termed "ecclesiastical" style. This emerges clearly in Matthew 23:1–12. Here the Pharisees are criticized because their interpretation of the law takes little or no account of human frailty and tends to be more severe than humane (v. 4). They are people who make custom their dictator, vanity and ostentation their lifestyle. Showing off, parading piety, enjoying the limelight, insisting on places of honor—these are forms of playacting, incredible performances in the name of religion (vv. 5–7). The admonition to leaders in Jesus' community is: You must remember that you are *servants* of the community. You must avoid the titles "rabbi," "father," "teacher." The title "rabbi"—literally, "my great one"—would sit incongruously on one who is "slave" (*doulos*) of the community. Nor is one to be addressed as "teacher"—practically the same as "rabbi." Not much elbowroom for clericalism! True religion as taught and exemplified by Jesus is a family-of-God affair, characterized by simplicity, affection, brother/sisterhood (vv. 8–12). There is only one Father, God, and all people are brothers and sisters. There ought not to be insistence on privilege and an exercise of power that distorts this relationship (see Mark 10:42–45).

TEMPLE

If Jesus was critical of sabbath observance, he was even more so of temple worship. The charge urged at the trial, that he had threatened to destroy the temple (see Mark 14:57), indicates that his critique of the temple priesthood was well known. The passage Mark 11:12–25 is an instructive instance of Jesus' stance. It is an example of Mark's sandwich technique: The account of the cleansing of the temple is "sandwiched" between the two phases of the fig tree narrative. The evangelist thereby signals that the stories should be understood in relation to each other. The curse (v. 21) becomes a judgment on the temple. On the way from Bethany to Jerusalem, a leafy tree seemed to promise fruit. A typically Markan explanatory phrase explains "It was not the time (literally, "season" [*kairos*]) for figs." This jarring note alerts us: we must look to a symbolic meaning. The temple tree, despite its leafy show, is barren at the *kairos* of its visitation. The Messiah "went to see" and found it fruitless.

The prophetic gesture of Jesus, his "cleansing" of the temple, symbolically disrupted the temple's cultic life. He is depicted as driving out those who offered for sale animals and birds and other commodities required for the sacrifices, the pilgrims who purchased them, and the moneychangers who exchanged the varied currency of the pilgrims for the Jewish or Tyrian coinage with which the temple tax must be paid. He prohibited the carrying of cultic vessels. It is inconceivable, particularly so near Passover with its influx of pilgrims, that Jesus could really have cleared the temple courts and brought the whole elaborate business to a standstill. His action, on a necessarily very limited scale, was a prophetic gesture, and would have been recognized as such (v. 18).

The motivation of his action is given in v. 17: It was God's intention that the temple should be a house of prayer "for all nations." This had not been achieved because the temple remained the jealously guarded preserve of Israel. Worse, the temple and its cult had become a "den of robbers," as the quotation from Jeremiah 7:8–11 makes plain. The temple and its service had become an escape hatch: The temple cult, it was felt, would automatically win forgiveness of ill behavior and bring about communion with God. In his emphatic rejection of this view, the prophet Jesus was in the line of Amos, Hosea, and Jeremiah (see Amos 4:4–5; 5:21–24; Hosea 5:1–2; 6:1–6; Jer 7:1–15; 26:1–19). In Jesus' view, because it was so abused, the temple cult had no longer any raison d'être. Its time had run out. The prophetic gesture presaged what his death was to achieve (15:38; see 13:2; 14:58; 15:29). The chief priests and the scribes had heard the message (see 11:28). They would not forget.

Coming after the episode of the cleansing of the temple, Peter's drawing of attention to the withered fig tree (vv. 30–31) serves to highlight the temple crisis. The temple and its cult are defunct. There is now another way to God, marked by faith (vv. 22–23), prayer (v. 24), and forgiveness

(v. 25). Henceforth, for Jesus' disciples, prayer takes the place of temple worship and marks a turn from places and practices that are no longer authentic. There is transition from a reserved temple to a house of prayer for all nations. The temple was the house of God. Jesus is now where God is to found (see John 4:21–23).

This is the meaning of the rending of the temple curtain from top to bottom at the death of Jesus (Mark 15:38). The temple had lost its significance. It was the end of the cult through which God had hitherto mediated forgiveness of sin and salvation. The temple curtain "was torn"—by God! Salvation is henceforth mediated uniquely through the shedding of his blood by the wholly faithful Son of God. Jesus had already said as much. He had done so in his words to his disciples. "For the Son of Man came not to be served but to serve, and to give his life as a ransom for many [all]" (10:45). And in his words at the Last Supper: "This is my blood of the covenant which is poured out for many [all]" (14:24). The temple is gone. God's Son is henceforth the "place" of salvation.

Compassion

Jesus displayed compassion throughout his mission. He consistently put people first.

In Mark 6:1–36 Jesus' attempt to find solitude for himself and his disciples was frustrated, but he was not annoyed. Instead, he was deeply touched by the earnestness of the crowd who had come to hear him and by their need: "He had compassion for them because they were like sheep without a shepherd" (v. 34). However, at the second feeding (Mark 8:1–9), Jesus was moved to compassion by the people's physical need: "I have compassion for the crowd, because they have been with me now for three days and they will faint on the way—and some of them have come from a great distance" (8:2–3).

Our gospels have two notably different versions of the beatitudes: Matthew 5:3–12 and Luke 6:20–23. Matthew has nine beatitudes. Luke has four—but with corresponding "woes" (Luke 6:24–26). Both versions grew from an original that goes back to Jesus, the additions and adaptations being due to the evangelists (or the traditions they had inherited). We can, without much trouble, discern a form of the beatitudes that would stand as a common basis for the development of the evangelists and that may reasonably be regarded as the beatitudes of Jesus. These are three:

Blessed are the poor, for the kingdom is theirs.
Blessed are those who hunger, for they will be filled.
Blessed are the afflicted, for they will be comforted.

The beatitudes do not refer to three different categories but to three aspects of the same distressful situation. The first sets the tone. In declaring the poor blessed, Jesus gives concrete expression to the good news that he brings to the poor. The other two beatitudes make precise, and develop, the content of the first. In the gospels, the poor are the indigent, those who depend totally on alms—they are the hungry, they are those who lament their unhappy lot. The most important text of the earliest Jesus tradition is this beatitude addressed to the poor. It is a fulfillment of Isaiah 61:1, "He has sent me to bring good news to the oppressed," a promise that the wretched lot of the poor will be reversed under the reign of God. In Palestine, poor Jews were coming together as disciples of Jesus. Their present experience of poverty, hunger, and tears played a decisive part in determining the object of their hope: they firmly expected that their lot would be reversed (see Luke 1:52–53). Jesus was hope of the poor.

NEIGHBOR

The introduction (Luke 10:25–28) is essential for an understanding of the parable of the good samaritan. The lawyer's question—"What must I do to inherit eternal life?"—was meant to embarrass Jesus. Jesus adroitly put the onus on his questioner, who found that his reply (from Deut 6:5) to Jesus' counter-question had won approval. The lawyer tried again and asked for a definition of "neighbor." This time he must have felt that the "Master" would be hard put to reply for he had raised what was, in fact, a much debated matter. The Essenes of Qumran, for instance, would maintain that all "sons of darkness," that is, all who did not belong to the sect, should be excluded. Others, less radical, would rule out "sinners." All would agree that, in the broadest interpretation, "neighbor" should be limited to Jews and proselytes. It is expected that Jesus, too, will respect the broad limits. It remains to be seen whether he will narrow them appreciably.

Though not explicitly stated, it is certainly implied that the man who was mugged on the road to Jericho was a Jew (v. 30). His nationality is not expressly mentioned because the point of the parable is that the lawyer's question is not going to be answered in terms of nationality or race. Priest and Levite refused to become involved in what, one way or other, would be a messy business (vv. 31–33). Jesus did not accuse them of callousness; he did not pass judgment on their conduct. They were men who lacked the courage to love. Dare we say they represent the common man? After the priest and Levite, it might be expected that the third

traveler—a series of three is typical of this kind of story—
would turn out to be a Jewish layman. The bias would be
anticlerical. The drama is that the third character, the hero
of the story, was one of the despised Samaritans. He has
been deliberately chosen to bring out the unselfishness of
love. This man gave first aid to the victim and carried him
to an inn. Whatever a cynic might have thought of his conduct thus far, the man turns out to be the realist. He did not
naively presume on the softheartedness of the innkeeper
but paid him in advance to look after the patient.

At the close, Jesus got the lawyer to answer his own
question—"The one who showed him mercy" (v. 37). Yet,
had he really responded to the original question? In v. 39
he had asked: "Who is my neighbor?" while the question
that Jesus puts to him is rather, "To whom am I neighbor"
(v. 36). The lawyer was concerned with the object of love
and his question implied a limitation: My neighbor is one
who belongs to such and such a group. Jesus looked to the
subject of love: Which of the three had acted as neighbor?
The lawyer's question was not answered because it was a
mistaken question. One may not determine theoretically
who one's neighbor is because love is not theory but practice. One's neighbor is any person who needs one's help,
says the parable. The wounded man was neighbor to all
three; the Samaritan alone was neighbor in return. The
story grew out of Jesus' own unlimited compassion: *He* is
the Good Samaritan!

"I WAS HUNGRY..."

In Matthew's last judgment scene (Matt 25:31–46),
the Son of Man is cast as a king who sits in judgment.
Largely through the influence of this passage, the image of

Christ as judge has had a profound—unhappy—effect on Christian tradition. This image of Christ is far from being the dominant one in the New Testament. And in our passage, when one looks closely, it will be seen that judgment is "auto-judgment": We judge ourselves by our omissions or our deeds. In the previous parables of chapters 24–25, Matthew had summoned to watchfulness, to readiness, to faithfulness. Now, in 25:31–46, he spells out what it means to be watchful and ready and faithful. It means being able to recognize the Son of Man in those in need, to translate this love into deeds of concern. There is the yardstick and by it one is measured.

To appreciate the passage rightly, one must understand that it is retrospective. Matthew has in mind how Jesus had comported himself—how he related to people. What Jesus did and said becomes the standard of judgment. He had come, a human being, into our human history, to tell us of the Godness of God: the *Deus humanissimus*, the God bent on the salvation of humankind. Jesus taught and lived that the reality of God is revealed in the realization of more humanity among fellow human beings—giving drink to the thirsty, feeding the hungry, welcoming the stranger. This story of judgment is focused on purely human concerns. But these are God's concern: "Come, you beloved of my Father." The emphasis is on the needy person, the one in distress. What is at stake in this last judgment is one's attitude toward the little ones, the humble and the needy. The criterion is not the standard of religion or cult. It is, starkly, has one helped those in need? It is compassion.

The truth is that the king who is judge of all is the crucified king, and he is met in everyone who suffers. It is because they had failed to understand Jesus' identification with the poor and suffering that the "goats" had failed to minister to him and to serve him. They had not loved the poor in concrete deeds of mercy. This Jesus, the crucified one, is the Son of Man who utters judgment—but what kind of judgment is this? He is the one who identifies himself with the lowly, with all the daughters and sons of humankind. A God bent on humankind, and nothing short of that, becomes the standard of our concern for those in need. That is why just this concern is the criterion of judgment. That is why the words of warning sound so harshly: "Depart from me, you cursed" (v. 41).

Immediately there is a problem. Can one, as a Christian, really believe that the suffering Jesus on the cross who prayed: "Father, forgive them, for they do not know what they do" (Luke 23:34) could, as risen Lord, declare in awful judgment: "Depart from me, you accursed, into the eternal fire"? Matthew, it seems (25:41), would have us think so. That such is really his intent becomes incredible when we understand that the "they" of Luke's text embraces all who brought Jesus to death. Jesus prays forgiveness of the obdurate chief priests and their allies. Luke is suggesting that even perpetrators of evil never really appreciate God's goodness or the strange wisdom of his purpose. Besides, we should see that seemingly inexorable sentence in Matthew against what we know of the God of the Old Testament and the New. He is the wondrously inconsistent God who "grieves in his heart" that he had ever made this complicated, stubborn, and treacherous human creature (Gen 6:5–8)—only to decide to put up with them henceforth (8:21). She is the God whose mother-heart recoils at the prospect of losing Ephraim (Hosea 11:8). He is the God who desires the salvation of all (1 Tim 2:4); he is the God who did not spare his own Son (John 3:16). Surely, Jesus would have us believe that his God and ours loves us with divine love that is beyond our human imagining.

In effect, the "last judgment" is a warning: It primarily relates to one's conduct in the present. One is challenged to live in such a manner so that, should it occur, one would not be caught unawares. We are being taught how we should prepare for the "coming" of the Lord, prepared for our meeting with him. The "last judgment" is taking place in my life here and now. The "books" are being written. But has my name "been written in the book of life since the foundation of the world" (Rev 17:8)? There is the true judgment. This man of Nazareth, who went about doing good, who died on a cross because he had espoused the cause of human freedom, will not have us see God as an inflexible judge. He would have us see the tears of a God who weeps in concert with human woe.

Forgiveness

Jesus ben Sirach had regarded the forgiveness of our neighbor as crucially important for right human conduct (Sirach 28:2–4). We should expect nothing less from Jesus of Nazareth. His stance is manifest in Matthew 18:21–35. Peter had come forward with a question: "Lord, if another member of the church sins against me, how often should I forgive? As many as seven times?" (v. 21). He was, indeed, being generous and, obviously, expected Jesus' approval. To his chagrin, the answer came: "Not seven times, but, I tell you, seventy times seven" (v. 22)—forgiveness without limit. The appended parable of the unforgiving servant (vv. 23–35) drives home the point. It also shifts the focus to God's forgiveness of sin.

The disparity between the sums cited in the parable of Matthew 18:23–35 is gigantic—ten thousand talents is an unimaginable amount. A debt, impossible to repay, is written off casually by the king, and the debtor is not even fired. It is the situation one finds in Luke 15:11–24. Yet one who had been shown such mercy cannot find it in his heart to remit a paltry debt. Not only that: He will not even give his fellow servant—his social equal—reasonable time and opportunity to repay. The king who had been moved with "pity" (v. 27) is now "angry" (v. 34).

The parable is a thinly veiled allegory. The "king" is a merciful God who freely and lovingly forgives sin. Luke has painted the warmer picture of prodigal father and wayward child (Luke 15:11–24). The reality is the same in either case. Like the younger son in the Lukan parable, this man, too, is forgiven with no strings attached. Faced with a cry of desperation, the forgiving God was moved with pity (Matt 15:27). But, when the recipient of such forgiveness cannot find it in his heart to be merciful, the master is angry (v. 33). Response to God's gracious forgiveness cannot be payment of a debt that is already fully remitted. It is, instead, warm thanksgiving for the blessing of such forgiving love. And the story in Matthew underlines again that sin, as God regards it, is man's inhumanity to man (even more sadly, man's inhumanity to woman), whatever shape that may take. Our abuse of others (and of ourselves) is an affront to the loving Father who counts us as his children. Jesus clearly understood this because he knew his Father. A corollary: Jesus asks us, frail humans, to be forgiving without limit. He dares to ask the impossible because he knew that his God is the Abba whose forgiveness literally knows no limit.

FRIEND OF SINNERS

In chapters 1–3 of the Letter to the Romans, the apostle Paul painted in stark colors the fate of humankind enslaved to *Hamartia*—Sin—sin personified. He did so as a foil to divine generosity: "God proves his love for us in that while we still were sinners Christ died for us" (Rom 5:8). The offer of God's forgiveness was distinctive of Jesus' ministry. Indeed, he won notoriety as "friend of sinners." Traditionally the challenge of Jesus has been modified in every conceivable manner. Here is a case in point. Jesus welcomed sinners—without condition. This was shockingly unconventional and a scandal to the righteous. Jesus was too much for the religious authorities of his day. He seems to be too much for the religious authorities of any day. Always, it seems, sinners can find the gap and encounter the gracious forgiveness and welcome of the Father/Mother—ever to the discomfiture of the righteous.

> "Why does he eat with tax collectors and sinners?"…"Those who are well have no need of a physician, but those who are sick; I come to call not the righteous but sinners" (Mark 2:16–17).

Jesus was the friend of sinners. The text witnesses to a conflict between the Jesus movement and other Jews on the issue. Jesus' reference to himself as "physician" implied more than a proverbial justification of his conduct. If he ate with sinners it was because the sick had need of the physician—they were not to be marginalized and avoided. For those who could see, his breaking bread with sinners was a declaration that the kingdom had indeed "come near" (1:15): the physician was at work.

The whole passage Mark 2:13–17 illustrates Jesus' attitude toward sinners and strikingly brings to the fore the fact that his concern for outcasts was a scandal to the religious-minded. Similarly, we may take it that those addressed in Matthew 21:31 ("Truly I say to you, the tax collectors and the harlots go into the kingdom of God before you") are Jews who deny to tax collectors and sinners the right to hope in God's forgiveness. The offense of the statement is its clear implication that the wretched prostitutes and detested tax collectors, scorned by the refined and the religious, are preferred by God to their despisers. Pharisees would be prepared to accept that God is merciful to sinners; they would not accept the unconditional forgiveness of God implicit in the role of Jesus. In the earliest Jesus movement the Pharisees are not representative of a Judaism hostile to Christianity. They are Jews who perceived that Jesus was making an enormous and, to them, unacceptable claim. He was claiming that God takes the part of the poor and the outcast—simply because they are poor, deprived, and despised. The rule of God was being inaugurated among the lowly and despised, not among the "righteous." This they could not and would not accept. At a further level, Jesus is rejecting any labeling or categorizing of people as "sinners."

The one distinctive note we can be certain marked Jesus' teaching about the kingdom is that it would include the "sinners." If we are truly to appreciate the scandal of the righteous at Jesus' befriending of sinners, we must understand who the sinners are. The term "sinners" in the Old Testament refers to people who, in some fundamental manner, stand outside the law. They are the "wicked" (*reshaim*). The Septuagint (the Greek Old Testament) rendered *reshaim* by *hamartóloi* ("sinners") and Greek-speaking Jews used the term to refer to the nonobservant who, it was maintained, had thereby placed themselves outside the covenant. The "sinners" of the gospels are these "wicked" people regarded as living, blatantly, outside the law. Jesus counted such within his fellowship. This was conduct that genuinely caused serious offense.

MERCY

Their Lukan setting (15:1–2) would fix the three parables of mercy (15:4–7, 8–10, 11–32) plausibly in the ministry of Jesus—one can claim no more. The "grumbling" of v. 2—"The Pharisees and the scribes were grumbling and saying, 'This fellow welcomes sinners and eats with them'"—says so much. The Pharisees had set the Torah as the way of righteousness—standing right with God—and had found in meticulous observance of it the achievement of righteousness. All who did not know the law, or who did not keep it, were "sinners," strangers to the path of righteousness. "But this crowd, which does not know the Law—they are accursed" (John 7:49). Jesus staunchly refused to categorize people; for him, no one was outcast. The Pharisees could not bear that Jesus welcomed sinners and sought them out. Worst of all, and there is a note of disgust, if not a tone of horror, he "eats with them" (see Luke 5:30; 7:34). What right had Jesus to flout so basic a requirement of the Torah?

Jesus countered their accusation by telling a parable (15:3)—in fact, three parables, the lost sheep, the lost coin, the lost son. His defense was that he sought out and welcomed the outcast because such is the Father's will. God is vindicator of the poor, the needy of any sort; the faithful Son was vindicator in turn. The outcasts, too, had caught his message. All their lives they had been told that they stood beyond the pale. They were without hope, robbed of hope by the "righteous." Only an infinitely gracious God can forgive the devastation visited, throughout history, by the "righteous" on "sinners," in particular by "righteous" with pastoral responsibility.

The plight of "outcasts" is well documented in the Pharisee and the Tax Collector (Luke 18:10–14). "The tax collector, standing far off, could not even look up to heaven, but was beating his breast and saying, 'God, be merciful to me, a sinner!' " In the end, he cannot really bring himself to accept that God was as the righteous had painted him. At least, he dared to hope that it was not so. Now, such as he are given glowing hope. This man of God, unlike the righteous, did not shun them. No wonder that "sinners" flocked to Jesus. And he, branded with the insult "friend of sinners," would have acknowledged this designation as the truest compliment. His meat was to do the will of him who sent him (John 4:34). Nothing was dearer to the Father's heart than this loving concern for the outcast.

Luke has a distinctive concern with repentance. In his gospel the words *repent* and *repentance* occur with notably more frequency than in Matthew and Mark. Compare Mark 2:17, "I have come to call not the righteous but sinners" with Luke 5:32, "I have come to call not the righteous but sinners to repentance," and Matthew 18:14, "it is not the will of your Father in heaven that one of these little ones should be lost," with Luke 15:7, "There will be more joy in heaven over one sinner who repents than over ninety-nine righteous persons who need no repentance." In short, repentance has a prominence in Luke–Acts that it does not have in the rest of the New Testament. When one looks beyond Luke it is evident that Jesus cannot be characterized as a preacher of repentance. He proclaimed the imminent coming of the kingdom as *salvation*. He focused not on repentance but on God's initiative.

This is not to say that Jesus was "soft" on sinners. He was, in fact, more radical than the reform-minded Baptizer. He did not seek to enforce the commandments of Jewish law. What he did do, and his claim was gravely offensive, was to assert the significance of his own mission and authority. He did not oppose the law, but he did indicate that accepting him and following him were more important than observance. His friendship with sinners was indeed an emphatic claim.

FORGIVENESS

John 8:1–11—the story of the woman taken in adultery—is out of place in the Fourth Gospel. In form and style it closely resembles the synoptic tradition. It would be quite at home in Luke. It seems to have been inserted in John because of the reference, in 7:51, to judgment according to the law.

The purpose of the scribes and Pharisees in bringing the adulteress to Jesus was to entrap him. If he pardoned her he could be accused of encouraging people to disobey the Law of Moses, which prescribed death by stoning for such conduct (Lev 20:10; Deut 13:9–10). In fact, as the Wisdom literature attests, that grim prescription had long been a dead letter, but the law could still be invoked as a challenge to Jesus. On the other hand, if he were to agree that she ought to be stoned to death, he would lose his reputation for mercy. Jesus deftly turned the challenge: Let the woman's accusers look to their own sins! He will not judge. Although the Father had granted full authority to his Son to pass judgment (John 5:22), Jesus really judges no one (8:15). His message is of mercy and forgiveness.

The story ends with the quiet scene of reconciliation between Jesus and the woman. The accusers had gone: Jesus alone remained to proclaim to her God's mercy. Augustine comments: *Relicti sunt duo—misera et misericordia*. Two stood there alone—wretchedness and mercy.

If there is the central reality of divine forgiveness, there is also the factor of human response to forgiveness. This is presented by Luke in an unforgettable manner. Nowhere more clearly than in Luke 7:36–50, the story of "a woman in the city, who was a sinner" (v. 37), do we see Jesus as Luke viewed him. The context, too, is perfect: Here indeed is the "friend of sinners" (v. 34). This story has links with other anointing stories: Mark 14:3–9; John 12:1–8—the story had assumed varied forms at the stage of oral tradition.

Here the Pharisee (Simon, v. 40), though he had invited Jesus to dine with him, had been coldly formal in the reception of his guest (vv.44–46). Though "sinner" has a wider connotation, the impression is that this woman was a prostitute and was well known as such (v. 30). Luke has courteously refrained from naming her and she remains anonymous. She was a woman who had previously encountered Jesus and had been assured by him of God's forgiveness. She had come to thank him, in a brave and extravagant manner. She, a woman and a sinner to boot, dared to crash this "stag party." She kissed and anointed the feet of a reclining Jesus, to the manifest scandal of his Pharisee host. Jesus, in contrast, acknowledged her presence and ministry with gentle courtesy. And his verdict was clear and to the point: "her great love proves that her sins have been forgiven" (v. 47). Simon's reasoning was: if Jesus were so unaware of the character of the woman that he had now incurred the ritual uncleanness of contact with a sinner, then he could not be the prophet whom many believed him to be.

The moneylender of Jesus' parable (vv. 41–43), who remits debts simply because his debtors were unable to pay, is hardly typical of his calling. It is manifest that close behind him stands a God who is ready to forgive any debts. Such is God, Jesus says, infinitely good and merciful. In the parable—"now which of them will love him more?" (v. 42)—"love" means thankful love, gratitude, so the question of Jesus would run: "Which of them would be the more grateful?" While Simon had omitted those gestures of esteem and affection with which an honored guest was received, the woman has prodigally supplied them (vv. 44–47). Simon is the target of the parable and is bluntly told: This woman, despite her sinful past, is closer to God than you, for she has what you lack: love and gratitude.

Crucified between two criminals, in the place called "The Skull," Jesus, with characteristic graciousness, prayed: "Father, forgive them; for they do not know what they are doing" (23:34). The "they" includes all who brought about his death. Jesus attributes ignorance to the obdurate priests and their Roman allies. Luke is suggesting that even perpetrators of evil never really appreciate God's goodness or the strange wisdom of his purpose. One of those crucified with Jesus asked him, directly: "Jesus, remember me when you come into your kingdom" (Luke 23:42). Typically, Jesus' response goes far beyond his expectation: "Truly, I tell you, today you will be with me in Paradise" (23:43). "Today" means this very day; to be with Jesus in "Paradise" is to be with Christ in the full presence of God. Jesus is friend of sinners to the end.

Nature

Jesus was a countryman who knew firsthand the life of the peasant farmer, of the vinedresser, and of the shepherd. His fisherman disciples introduced him to fishing practices on the Sea of Galilee. His love of nature shines through his words and images.

FARMING

The farmer of Mark 4:1–8 sowed haphazardly. While grains and seedlings and young plants in unfavorable circumstances perished, seed in good soil flourished. The smallness of the mustard seed plant was proverbial (Matt 17:20). Along the Sea of Galilee the mustard plant spread rapidly and could grow up to six feet. In the parable of Mark 4:26–29, which is proper to Mark, the farmer sowed, then bided his time until harvest. The seed sprouted and grew, without him taking anxious thought. The work of a farmer might be maliciously hampered—the parable of the Weeds among the Wheat (Matt 13:26–30). An enemy had scattered weed seeds in his victim's freshly seeded wheat field. The Greek *zizanion* names a noxious weed that, in its early stages, closely resembles the young wheat blade and cannot be readily distinguished from it. A fig tree requires special care (Luke 13:6–9). Unlike most trees in Palestine, the fig tree sheds its leaves in winter. Its budding and new leaves in spring are a sign that summer is not far off (Mark 13:28).

VINEYARD

The parable of Mark 12:1–12 displays precise knowledge of viniculture. "A man planted a vineyard, put a fence around it, dug a pit for the wine press, and built a watchtower" (12:1). The hedgerow was intended to keep animals out of the vineyard. The purpose of the wine press is obvious. The tower served both as lookout and shelter. In John 15:1–11 the Father is the vinegrower and Jesus is the *alethinos*, the genuine vine. Believers are branches of him, drawing life from him. As for wine, Jesus provided with generous abandon for the wedding guests at Cana (John 2:1–11). Wine was granted abiding significance: "Then he took a cup, and after giving thanks he gave it to them, and all of them drank from it" (Mark 14:23).

SHEPHERD

Mixed flocks of sheep and goats were commonplace in Palestine. At evening the shepherd separated the sheep from the goats. Since sheep are the more valuable, they are given preference in the parable of Matthew 25:31–33. Sheep were herded into a sheepfold at night. This sheepfold was a courtyard, or a walled enclosure in a field, and the sheep of various shepherds were corralled within. There was a proper approach to sheep herded in a sheepfold—through the gate opened by a keeper. Any other means of entry was path of a thief. Then there was the shepherd. He knew his sheep by name. When he called them, they followed him confidently (John 10:1–18).

FISHING

Four lake fishermen, while engaged in mending nets, were summoned to become fishers of people (Mark 1:16–20). Luke dramatized this call of the first disciples (Luke 2:1–11). A fishing net catches fish indiscriminately; later, the fishermen separate good from bad (Matt 13:47–48). Fishermen know how to manage boats and learn to cope with weather conditions. Caught in a severe storm on the lake—"waves beat into the boat, so that the boat was already being swamped"—experienced sailors panicked, while the "landlubber" Jesus calmly slept (Mark 4:37–38)! The tradesman Jesus would not have had practical experience of boats and fishing before the days of his lakeside mission. He was a fast learner and was able to give his fisherman friends lessons in their own craft. A fruitless night had left them ruefully washing empty nets. Next day, when he was done using one of a pair of boats as an improvised pulpit, he bade them push out into deeper water and cast their nets. They struck a shoal almost beyond their ability to cope (Luke 5:3–7). As risen Lord he would again advise them: "Cast the net to the right side of the boat and you will find some!" (John 21:6).

WEATHER

Jesus had a sensitivity to weather conditions characteristic of countrymen (and fishermen). At evening: "It will be fair weather, for the sky is red." At morning: "It will be stormy today, for the sky is red and threatening" (Matt 16:2–3). Again, a cloud rising in the west is sign of rain; a south wind brings scorching heat (Luke 12:54–58). He enjoyed the antics of little birds and found pleasure in wild flowers (Matt 6:26–28). There is the charming image of Jesus himself as a mother hen gathering her brood under her wings (Luke 13:34).

In short, Jesus of Nazareth lived in the Palestinian world of his day and was, as any mature person is, responsive to his environment.

Humor

It ought not to surprise that Jesus had a refined sense of humor. This emerges notably in his parables. The sower of Mark 4:3–7 had sowed haphazardly: on a busy pathway, on rocks, among thorns. Farmers would have scoffed at his stupidity. Jesus' hearers would have chuckled at the ludicrous picture of a man going about with a two-by-four sticking out of his eye as he peered to spot a speck in the eye of another (Matt 7:1–5). And there was that housebuilder who sought a shortcut. The floor of a *wadi*, a dry riverbed, looked promising. Nice and level, and stones conveniently all about. He went ahead and built. The hearers would have laughed: What a nut! The winter floods would teach him a painful lesson (Matt 7:24–27).

In Luke 11:5–8 the suggestion of stubborn deafness to a friend's insistent request would have met with shocked disbelief: What boor would behave in such a disgraceful manner? The gutsy widow (Luke 18:2–8) would have won a round of applause. Judges would not have been popular among a struggling peasant population—it was too well known that they favored the rich. This widow had worn one down by sheer pestering. Good for her!

In Mark 7:24–30 the focus of the story is the dialogue between Jesus and the Gentile woman. She earnestly begged Jesus to heal her daughter. He refused because, as he told her, the rules did not permit it: "It is not fair to take the children's food and throw it to the dogs" (v. 27). Jesus acknowledged the distinction between Jew and Gentile. The woman will not be put off by Jesus' refusal: all very well, indeed—but even the dogs get crumbs! Jesus must have laughed. He had been trumped. This quick-witted woman had appealed to his sense of humor. He assured her that she need have no further worry: her sick daughter was well again.

Jesus' hearers must have appreciated the parable of the steward (Luke 16:1–8). They would have enjoyed the humor of his bold characterization: his putting forward of a rascal as a spur to resolute decision and action. The manager (steward) had been accused of embezzlement. Until he produced his books he had a breathing space. He rewrote contracts in favor of his master's creditors and in hope of a kickback. It was a neat scam! The master, who had to honor the contracts duly made in his name, ruefully applauded the resourceful conduct of his unscrupulous manager. Jesus' outrageous story would have caught the attention of his hearers. His hope was that they would have caught his message: that his disciples show as much resourcefulness in God's business as men of the world do in their affairs.

Two other instances: The disciples were in a boat at evening, far out on a stormy lake (Matt 14:22–27). Suddenly, Jesus appeared, walking toward them on the waters of the lake. Peter, with bravado, offered to step out to meet him. Jesus bade him, "Come." Peter started out across the water, quickly panicked, and cried for help. Jesus must have smiled, with a shake of the head: typical Peter! And at Bethany, Jesus would certainly have smiled at Martha's scolding—"Lord, do you not care that my sister has left me to do all the work by myself? Tell her then to help me" (Luke 10:40)—smiled because he knew his dear friend so well.

Exasperation

Jesus had come "not to be served but to serve, and to give his life a ransom for many [all]" (Mark 10:45). He reached out to all, offered salvation to all. For him, no one was outcast, beyond the range of God's mercy. He was consistently patient in his dealings with those classified as "sinners." He gladly broke bread with them (see Luke 15:1). There were those who would not listen, in particular, those who should have known better. With such he could, and did, display exasperation.

Jesus' experience of rejection in his hometown of Nazareth (Mark 6:1–6) lays bare one of the roots of unbelief. Jesus' townsfolk reacted with initial surprise. They were on the verge of asking the right questions about him. But they made the mistake of imagining that they already had the answers to their own questions. Besides, there was the scandal of Jesus' ordinariness; they could not bring themselves to acknowledge the greatness or the mission of a man who was one of themselves. They "took offense" at him. Pained by rejection, "he was amazed at their unbelief" (v. 6a).

OPPONENTS

Jesus had regular dialogue with Pharisees. While they shared common ground, they had serious theological differences. At times, his impatience with them showed. This is apparent elsewhere in this study. Here we look at the more direct instances. A case in point is the Pharisees' demand of a "sign from heaven," designed to test Jesus (Mark 8:11–13). "He sighed deeply": his reaction expressed deep emotion and indignation (see 3:5). It was a sigh in which anger and sorrow both had part. "No sign will be given"—the Greek formula (*ei dothēsetai*) is, in fact, an imprecation: "May I die if God grants this generation a sign" (the passive designates God as agent). The refusal could not be more absolute. "He left them" (v. 13) because there was no scope for his ministry among them.

In the passage on self-deception (Matt 7:21–23) Jesus' words of condemnation are strong and unexpected: "I never knew you; go away from me, you evildoers" (v. 23). "Knowledge," in the Bible, is often the knowledge of personal relationship. It has overtones of love and attachment. Here ostensibly religious people have claimed to have acted in the name of Jesus. Caught in the web of their own religious system, they have never truly known him. The essential demand was to do the will of God (v. 21). In this they had failed. In Matthew 11:20–24 Jesus reproached three Galilean towns for their failure to respond with repentance to Jesus' deeds of power. On Judgment Day things will go better, not only for Tyre and Sidon, but even for Sodom than for them! A stern warning indeed—in judgment guise.

The little parable of Luke 7:31–35 is introduced by the observation (v. 30) that "the Pharisees and the lawyers," by refusing John's baptism, had effectively rejected God's purpose for themselves. The children in question, *sitting* in the marketplace—the boys playing the flute and the girls chanting a funeral dirge—formed part of a game. The remaining boys were expected to dance the wedding dance (the round dance at weddings was performed by men) and the rest of the girls ought to have formed a funeral procession. Since both groups had failed to do so, those who had initiated the game complained that they were spoilsports. The point of the parable, then, is the frivolous capriciousness of those children. The conduct of the scribes and Pharisees is no better. They will listen neither to the Baptist nor to Jesus. They are plain stubborn!

Jesus also experienced disappointment. This shows in the episode of the ten lepers (Luke 17:11–19): "Were not ten made clean? But the other nine, where are they?" (v. 17). His disappointment, however, was not because the nine failed to thank *him*. "Was none of them found to return and give praise *to God* except this foreigner?" (v. 18).

DISCIPLES

Jesus had chosen his own disciples. He earnestly desired them to be faithful disciples. Again and again they failed. Relations between Jesus and his disciples are at their most tense in the Gospel of Mark. Time and again his exasperation shows.

In the episode of the stilling of the lake storm (Mark 4:37–41) the disciples display the disrespect typical of them in Mark and rebuke Jesus: "Teacher, do you not care that we are perishing?" (v. 38). He rebuked them in turn: "Why are you afraid? Have you no faith?" (v. 40). The term *deiloi,* "afraid," is very strong, expressing total disarray. During the storm the disciples had failed in that trust in God of which the tranquil sleep of Jesus (v. 38) was a visible sign. He accused them, especially, of lack of trust in him. Throughout the first half of his gospel, Mark had stressed the failure of the Twelve to understand (4:13, 40–41; 6:51; 7:18; 8:4). In all cases they displayed lack of spiritual insight in their failure to discern the hidden meaning in a word or deed of Jesus. The passage 8:14–21 is the climax of this theme at this stage. A series of seven rhetorical questions conveys Jesus' bitter disappointment at their tardiness. "Do you not yet understand?" is the burden of this censure.

In response to the question "Who do you say that I am?" Peter had acknowledged Jesus to be the Messiah (8:29). Jesus expounded his understanding of Messiahship: "The Son of Man must undergo great suffering, and be rejected by the elders, the chief priests and the scribes, and be killed..." (8:31). "And Peter took him aside..." (v. 32): We can picture him, in his earnestness, taking hold of Jesus and rebuking him: "I have said you are the Messiah, haven't I? Why this nonsense about suffering and death?" He seemed, for the moment, to have forgotten who was Master and who disciple. Peter would have shared the current messianic expectation, based on the promise to David in 2 Samuel 7. The Messiah, son of David, would come from God in royal splendor, to inaugurate the kingdom of God, the universal rule of God. The Messiah, most certainly, would not die. The notion of a suffering Messiah was foreign to Peter. His confession, "You are the Messiah," is a classic example of "verbal orthodoxy": The formula is correct, but the understanding of it is quite mistaken. Jesus' rebuke of Peter was severe: "Get behind me, Satan!"—the words recall Matthew 4:10, "Begone, Satan!" The temptation in the wilderness (Matt 4:1–11) aimed at getting Jesus to conform to the popularly envisaged messianic role. Peter's acknowledgement of Jesus as Messiah had, in principle, set him apart from "people" (Mark 8:27), but now he found himself rebuked for judging in an all-too-human way. Peter, and all like him, who set their minds on "human things" stand opposed to God's purpose and align themselves with Satan.

In the absence of Jesus (and the inner circle of Peter, James, and John) on the mount of transfiguration (Mark 9:2–8), the remaining disciples proved unable to heal an epileptic boy (9:18–19). "They were not able"—Mark underlines the disciples' inability: not only the petitioner but they themselves (v. 28) were surprised to find that they were powerless. After all, they had been granted power over unclean spirits (6:7, 13); their previous success (see 6:30) had gone to their heads. Jesus reacted in stark terms: "You faithless generation, how much longer must I be among you? How much longer must I put up with you?" (v. 19). The reproof is general and expresses the weariness of Jesus in face of the lack of faith manifested by his contemporaries—in particular, the disciples.

Very soon these disciples would again incur the displeasure of Jesus. In 10:13–16 Mark has delightfully brought a little scene to life: mothers eager to present their children to the renowned rabbi and wonder-worker; the disciples officiously intervening; Jesus indignant at their rebuff to children; his taking them into his arms (see 9:36). His word was peremptory: "Let the little children come to me; do not stop them!" (v. 14).

"Little ones" crop up in Matthew 18:6–7, now not as children but as "these little ones who believe in me": the humblest members of a Christian community, the vulnerable. Jesus sternly warns any who would put a "stumbling block" in their path. He stressed the grievousness of the sin of those who lead simple Christians astray by callously disturbing their fragile faith. They deserve death by drowning—a Roman punishment particularly repugnant to Jews because of lack of proper burial. The "great millstone" would preclude recovery of the body. The warning, then, is very severe.

On his way to Jerusalem, Jesus and his disciples were denied hospitality in a Samaritan village (Luke 9:51–56). James and John, living up to their reputation as "sons of thunder" (Mark 3:17), want to do an Elijah-act (see 2 Kings 1:10–12): "Lord, do you want us to command fire to come down from heaven and consume them?" (Luke 9:54). Jesus turned and rebuked them (v. 55). Some manuscripts of the Gospel carry a relevant comment: "You do not know what spirit you are of; for the Son of Man has not come to destroy the lives of human beings but to save them." In John 21:20–23 Peter is true to form, still the impetuous one. In boldly asking about the fate of the Beloved Disciple he had moved beyond the bounds of propriety. This is no business of his! The risen Lord is firm: "as for you, *you* follow me!"

And there is Jesus' disappointment. With the disciples at Gethsemane: "Simon, are you asleep? Could you not keep awake one hour?" (Mark 14:37). "Are you still sleeping and taking your rest?" (v. 41). Disappointment with family: his family "went out to restrain him, for people were saying, 'he has gone out of his mind' " (Mark 3:21). And the significant comment in John 7:5: "For not even his brothers believed in him." The pain he had felt at rejection in his hometown (Mark 6:1–6) was compounded by the incomprehension of his family.

There is the other side. If there is momentary impatience, there is also inexhaustible patience. It is a pattern manifest in the Old Testament, summed up in Isaiah 56:8:

> In overflowing wrath *for a moment* I hid my face
>   from you,
> but with *everlasting love* I will have compassion
>   on you,
> says the Lord, your Redeemer.

Like Father, like Son!

Anger

The passage Mark 1:40–45, the cleansing of the leper, sits lightly in its Markan context. We may discern, in the then-current attitude toward leprosy, a reason for the evangelist's insertion of it at this point. *Leprosy*, a word that in the Bible covers a variety of skin diseases (see Leviticus 13), was regarded as the ultimate uncleanness, which cut the afflicted one off from the community as a source of ritual defilement for others. Significantly, in the New Testament, the removal of leprosy is not described as healing but as cleansing. The law was helpless in regard to leprosy; it could only defend the community against the leper. But what the law could not achieve, Jesus accomplished.

According to the more widely attested reading, Jesus was moved with "pity" at the petition of the wretched man (v. 41). There can be little doubt that "moved with anger," not nearly so well attested, is the original reading. It is easy to understand why copyists would have changed it to "moved with pity"; it is incredible that they should have done the reverse. The anger of Jesus was twofold. It was his reaction to a disease that brought him face to face with the ravages of evil—all disease, it was thought, was caused by evil forces. More deeply it was because the unfortunate man had been branded a pariah. His disease had cut him off from social and religious life. Child of God, he was not permitted to come into the presence of God. If one were to touch him—even his garment—one became "unclean," unworthy to approach God. Thus can religion distort the graciousness of God. Jesus stepped forward, reached out, and firmly laid his hand on the man—no concern with uncleanness there! He was healed. The law (Lev 14:2–32) specified that one who claimed to be healed of leprosy should have the cure verified by a priest. In bidding the man to carry out the prescription, Jesus intended something more. "As a testimony to them" (v. 44) is to be taken as a challenge to the priesthood and their view of things—

it is testimony against them (see 6:11). Jesus was already aware that the priests did not look kindly upon his mission. Who are the lepers, the outcasts of our day? One readily thinks of, among others, those suffering from AIDS. Does one need to ask how Jesus would treat them? He would surely be "moved with anger" at how unkindly they are categorized by some "Christians."

Jesus had been carrying out his mission in Galilee: teaching, healing, exorcizing. Soon came confrontation with various opponents. It is documented in a series of five conflicts (Mark 2:1—3:6). The fifth conflict (3:1–6) is the climax of the series. Here Jesus himself is more aggressive and the plot against him (v. 6) points to the inevitable end of the persistent hostility. A trap had been set for Jesus: A man with a withered hand was positioned prominently in the synagogue. Jesus was angry. They were callously using this poor man as bait. One does not treat people so! They were making a mockery of the sabbath. He healed the man. The Pharisees promptly accused Jesus of an infringement of sabbath observance. He viewed the matter in a wholly different light and challenged their attitude. In forbidding healing on the sabbath, the rabbis would equivalently admit that, on this day, moral values were reversed: it was forbidden to "do good" and prescribed to "do evil"! For Jesus, the real issue is no longer what one is permitted to do. It is the obligation of doing good at all times and in all circumstances. Jesus asked: "Is it lawful to do good or to do harm on the sabbath, to save life or to kill?" How sad that the spirit of legalism has so regularly and so firmly asserted itself in the Christian church. We have been so zealous in multiplying rules and imposing them, so anxious to measure our Christianity by the punctiliousness of our "observance."

Much of what we have above noted under the heading *Exasperation* might readily fit under the title *Anger*. It is not superfluous to note some examples here. When Pharisees demanded a sign, Jesus was angered by their stubbornness—"He sighed deeply in his spirit" and categorically refused to perform any sign (Mark 8:12). Their slavish adherence to "the tradition of the elders" called forth his indignant accusation: You hypocrites! "You have a fine way of rejecting the commandment of God in order to keep your tradition" (7:9). Descending from the mount of transfiguration, he reacted to their general lack of faith in words tinged with anger: "You faithless generation, how much longer must I be among you? How much longer must I put up with you?" (9:19). Disciples, too, were part of the target. They earn again the rebuke of Jesus at their disregard for children. They had tried to put a stop to parents bringing little children for Jesus' blessing (10:13): "When Jesus saw this, he was indignant." When some were angry at what they regarded as criminal waste in a woman's gesture of anointing Jesus and scolded her (14:4–5), Jesus rounded on them: "Let her alone; why do you trouble her?" (v. 6). And the zealous James and John got their knuckles rapped in response to their demand for punishment of a Samaritan village that had refused hospitality (Luke 9:51–56). "He turned and rebuked them" (v. 55).

The cleansing of a leper (Mark 1:40–45) highlights Jesus' predilection for outcasts. His anger at the situation was a facet of his impatience with a religious stance that put observance before people. The point was made more sharply in the synagogue incident (3:1–6). A cripple was callously used as bait: what will Jesus do? He was angered by the shameful exploitation of a human being. He was angered by a stultifying legalism that would outlaw a good deed—on the sabbath! He had stressed from the first that all people should be respected. In regard to the sabbath, he had insisted that it was God's gift to humankind. It had been perverted into a burden (Mark 2:27). Jesus was critical of the religious observance of his day. It is not in doubt that he would be no less scathing today of any religious system that would confine the growth of people, that would seek to define religion in terms of "observance." His word stands: Religion is for men and women, not men and women for religion.

Fear

Fear is an inescapable human experience. It has been well said that true bravery is not in fearlessness but in steadfast coping with one's fear. Jesus knew fear—as two gospel passages attest. In a Johannine passage that has echoes of the synoptics' Gethsemane accounts, Jesus is apprehensive at the imminence of "the hour": "Now my soul is troubled. And what should I say—'Father, save me from this hour?' No, it is for this reason that I have come to this hour" (John 12:27). Jesus had previously declared: "The hour has come for the Son of Man to be glorified"— to be revealed (v. 23). Now he realizes that the "glorification," the revelation, will be on the cross. The hour of exaltation is also the hour of suffering, and Jesus feels terror at the prospect. He finds comfort in the assurance that the Father, whose will he had come to serve, will see him through it. And he receives that assurance (v. 28).

Mark's Gethsemane scene (Mark 14:32–42) is more harrowing. It shows that Jesus did not fully understand God's way, shows that he did not want to die. He prayed: "Father, for you all things are possible; remove this cup from me" (v. 36). While we may plausibly assert that *Abba* was

Jesus' preferred address to his God, the word *abba* occurs only once in the gospels—here in Mark 14:36. Its occurrence here is fitting: The familiar title seems to be wrested from Jesus at this awful moment. He prayed, explicitly that the cup be taken from him. He did not contemplate suffering and a horrible death with stoic calm. He was appalled at the prospect. He knew fear; Mark's language in vv. 33–34 is very strong. Jesus was brave as he rose above his dread to embrace what his God asked. But he must know if the path that opened before him was indeed the way that God would have him walk. He found assurance in prayer: The utterance of his trustful "Abba" already included "thy will be done." His prayer did not go unanswered, though the answer was paradoxical. As the Letter to the Hebrews puts it: "He was heard because of his reverent submission" (5:7). The obedient Son cried out to the Father and put himself wholly in the hands of the Father.

If Jesus said of the disciples, "the spirit is willing, but the flesh is weak" (Mark 14:38), that statement is not irrelevant to his own situation. Jesus himself had experienced human vulnerability: distress, agitation, and grief even to the point of death, to the point of asking the Father that the hour might pass him by and the cup be taken away. "Hour" and "cup" indicate the historical moment and the imminent prospect of fearsome death. But this, too, was the eschatological hour of the final struggle, the great *peirasmos*, "trial," before the triumph of God's kingdom. "The Son of Man is given over to the hands of sinners" (v. 41). In the Old Testament, God gives over the wicked to punishment; here, in contrast, a just man is "given over" by God—"my ways are not your ways" (Isa 55:8). Comfortingly, at the end, Jesus invited his disciples: "Get up, let *us* be going." Jesus still includes his disciples, even though they had failed him.

4

JESUS OF NAZARETH: REACTION

"THIS CHILD IS DESTINED for the falling and the rising of many in Israel, and to be a sign that will be opposed" (Luke 2:34).

The prophetic words of Simeon in Luke's infancy narrative really reflect later Christian knowledge of the historical mission of Jesus. Though he had come as the savior of his people (v. 11), he would be rejected by many of them (see John 1:11), for he would stand as a sign of contradiction, a stone that can be stumbling block or cornerstone depending on whether people turn their backs on him or accept him (see Luke 20:17–18; Acts 4:11; Rom 9:33; 1 Pet 2:6–8). In his presence there can be no neutrality, for he is the light that people cannot ignore (see John 9:39; 12:44–50), the light that reveals their inmost thoughts and forces them to take their part for him or against him.

Acceptance

MISSION TO HIS OWN PEOPLE

"I was sent only to the lost sheep of the house of Israel" (Matt 15:24).

Jesus' mission was to his own people. To them he proclaimed the kingdom of God, the rule of God, not alone in words but in his deeds of healing. The gospels assert that Jesus regularly attracted large crowds. It would appear that, on the whole, he met a favorable reception. It is not surprising that his healing ministry would have been warmly welcomed. Paradoxically, popular acclaim may have contributed to his death. This popularity was viewed by religious and political authorities as a threat. His teaching would not have been palatable to them. If he had spoken to deaf ears, it might not have mattered. But he had a following. That was dangerous.

How deep ran the commitment of the "crowds" we cannot say. Popular enthusiasm, as politicians know only too well, is fickle and ephemeral. Whether or not the ease with which the temple priests were able to turn the "crowd" against Jesus (see Matt 27:20–23) is strictly historical, it is credible. Crowds had flocked to hear Jesus. There was no crowd to protest his crucifixion. Jesus was neither the first nor the last courageous prophetic figure to suffer a like fate. "Like us in all things," indeed.

DISCIPLES

There were those who "followed" Jesus because they were called by him. These were "disciples." It is noteworthy that the word *mathétés*, "disciple," which occurs frequently in the gospels and Acts, is absent from the rest of the New Testament. It is associated with the mission of Jesus. And it carries a specific meaning. Distinctive features of this initial discipleship were: Jesus took the initiative in calling; "following" meant literal, physical following of an itinerant preacher; disciples were warned that they might face hostility and suffering. The evidence is clear that women, too, followed Jesus during his mission in Galilee and accompanied him on his last journey to Jerusalem (see Mark 15:40–41). This is wholly in keeping with Jesus' high regard for women.

From his disciples Jesus chose a core group—the Twelve (Mark 6:7). They symbolized the regathering, at the end of time of all the twelve tribes of Israel. The choice of the Twelve was a prophetic proclamation that God would reestablish his chosen people. After a single move to complete the number following the departure of Judas (Acts 1:15–26), it was quickly understood that the role of the Twelve was symbolic and pertained to the eschatological mission of Jesus himself. The Twelve, as such, had no role in the early church. Misleading deductions have been made from the fact that the Twelve were men. Indeed, Jesus had no choice. The Twelve symbolized Israel: twelve tribes descended from the twelve sons of Judah. They had to be men—the symbolism was fixed. What matters is that Jesus had chosen women, too, as his disciples.

There were also supporters of Jesus who had not been called to leave all and follow him. Some of them, men and women, are named in the gospels: Lazarus, Zacchaeus, Martha, and Mary. Surely there would have been others from among those who had been healed by Jesus. There was, then, within Israel, a solid core of those who would, after Easter, joyfully proclaim their faith in the risen Lord.

Opposition

Jesus was not welcomed by all. On the gospel evidence, he was constantly hassled by the Pharisees. Who were those Pharisees? They seem to have originated as a religious and political response to the program of Hellenization launched by Antiochus IV (175–163 BC), ruler of the Seleucid kingdom that included Palestine, and his Jewish supporters. The Pharisees perceived in this policy a threat to the very survival of the Jews as a distinct ethnic, cultural, and religious entity. They emphasized detailed study and observance of the Law of Moses. They also possessed a normative body of tradition—the traditions of the "fathers" or "elders." While they acknowledged that some of these legal rules and practices went beyond the law, they maintained that such practices were nevertheless God's word for Israel. They actively engaged in striving to convince ordinary Jews to observe these Pharisaic practices in their daily lives. Much of what is attributed to Pharisaic teaching refers to legal rulings or opinions regarding concrete behavior (*halakoth*) in matters of purity rules, sabbath observance, marriage and divorce. After AD 70 and the destruction of the temple by the Romans, as practically the only religious group to have survived the Jewish War, their influence would have increased.

All four gospels attest to Jesus' frequent contact with Pharisees throughout his mission. Though they had much in common, their relationship was, not surprisingly, tense, because they both addressed the same constituency. They both sought to influence the main body of Palestinian Jews and win them to their respective visions of what God was calling Israel to be. Jesus would have challenged them directly and in parable. In prophetic mode, he may have pronounced "woes" against them. Yet, the gospels acknowledge that some Pharisees were willing to give Jesus a serious hearing (e.g., Luke 7:36–50; John 3:1–2). Their relationship would have been notably less hostile than that represented in Matthew 23. As it stands, this is an indictment of Pharisaic Judaism painfully reflecting the bitter estrangement of church and synagogue toward the close of the first century AD. It is significant that Pharisees are practically absent from all passion narratives. The death of Jesus was brought about, historically, not by Pharisees, but by an alliance of the Jerusalem priesthood and Roman political authority.

In the gospels, "scribes" are regularly associated with Pharisees as well as with the priesthood. In Jesus' day, Palestinian scribes were bureaucrats. In Jerusalem, they assisted the priests in judicial proceedings in the council— the Sanhedrin. Their role was secretarial but, as in a modern civil service, some might have had a measure of influence. The gospels suggest that the scribes, as a homogenous group, formed part of a united front against Jesus. This is not historical.[1]

Rejection

Priests were most active in the passion narratives. Indeed, the gospels give the impression that the priestly aristocracy was principally involved in bringing Jesus to his death. The temple priests would have had little interest in a Galilean layman until they began to look upon him as a threat. Jesus' critique of the temple emerged as an accusation at his trial. His prophetic gesture in "cleansing" the temple (Mark 11:15–17) was very well understood: "When the chief priests and the scribes heard it, they kept looking for a way to kill him" (v. 18). Luke tells us (Acts 7) that his critique of the temple sealed Stephen's fate. It is hazardous to challenge entrenched religion. There was also the charge of "blasphemy" (Mark 14:64). However the high priest understood the term, he was branding Jesus as a heretic and deserving of death. He was, besides, a messianic pretender (vv. 61–62).

There was the threatening specter of a messianic uprising and consequent trouble with Rome. The Fourth Gospel voices the fear: "This man is performing many signs. If we let him go on like this, everyone will believe in him, and the Romans will come and destroy both our holy place and our nation" (11:47–48). The high priest Caiaphas gives voice to cynical political expediency: "You know nothing at all! You do not understand that it is better for you to have one man die for the people than to have the whole nation destroyed" (vv. 49–50).

This heretic and politically dangerous man had to go—an all-too-human situation. The snag was that the Sanhedrin could not carry out a death sentence. The Romans had to be involved (see John 18:31). The messianic title "King of the Jews," which runs through all four passion narratives, served their purpose: It could be given blatantly political emphasis. In Pilate's eyes, a claim to be king independently of Roman approval was high treason. The temple priests won Roman sanction and the fate of Jesus was sealed.

"It was nine o'clock in the morning when they crucified him" (Mark 15:25). Death by crucifixion was intentionally degrading. Even the choice of the place of Jesus' execution was a calculated insult. Archaeological research has shown that Golgotha, a disused quarry, was a refuse dump at the time. There was no majesty in the death of Jesus, no trace of glory. Mark describes a sudden, violent death: "Jesus gave a loud cry and breathed his last" (15:34). He had cried out, in agony, "My God, my God, why have you forsaken me?" Jesus died abandoned by his disciples, alone, in agony. "No New Testament text more boldly expresses the reality of Jesus' humanity or the manner of his dying."[2]

In Roman eyes Jesus was a duly executed criminal; disposal of the body was the business of the Roman authorities. Joseph of Arimathea, a Torah-observant Sanhedrin member, was concerned to fulfill the law—here that the body of one crucified should not be left overnight on the tree (Deut 21:23). He approached Pilate and was duly granted the corpse of Jesus (Mark 15:42–44). It would be a hasty, dishonorable burial of one executed on a charge of blasphemy—as the sanhedrist Joseph would have assessed it. The body was not anointed; it was simply wrapped in a linen shroud and placed in a niche of that disused quarry. Large stones would have closed it off.

5

JESUS OF NAZARETH: TRIUMPH OF FAILURE

IN SOME RESPECTS THE painful Gethsemane episode (Mark 14:32–42) is the most comforting in the gospels. There we see Jesus at his most vulnerably human. Hitherto, he had marched resolutely to meet his fate. Now that the dreadful moment is upon him, "he began to be distressed and agitated" (v. 33). Jesus was shattered.

Triumph of Failure

It had been dawning on Jesus what the Father seemed to be asking of him. He needed assurance that what God seemed to ask, he really did ask: "Abba, Father, for you all things are possible, remove this cup from me; yet, not what I want but what you want" (Mark 14:36). He explicitly prayed that the cup be taken from him. He did not contemplate suffering and death with stoic calm. He was appalled at the prospect. He knew fear. He was brave as he rose above his dread to embrace what the Father asked. But he must know if the path that opened before him was indeed the way his God would have him walk. He found assurance in prayer (14:35, 36, 39). His prayer did not go unanswered. As the Letter to the Hebrews puts it: "He was heard because of his reverent submission" (Heb 5:7). That answer was: No! In traditional biblical imagery, Luke has dramatized the heavenly response: "Then an angel from heaven appeared to him and gave him strength" (Luke 22:53). Jesus was assured that it was indeed the Father's will that he tread the lonely road of total rejection. Not the Father's will as part of some cold, inflexible design. The Father was prepared to make a supreme sacrifice; "Surely, they will respect my Son!" (Mark 12:6). Jesus had understood that just here lay the victory over evil. For evil is finally helpless before a love that will never cry: Enough!

Failure?

The truth is that his death marked Jesus as a failure. Jesus was executed on the order of a Roman provincial official. An alleged troublemaker in that bothersome province of Judea had been dealt with. The incident did not cause a ripple in imperial affairs. Yet history has shown that this execution was an event of historic proportions. Its ripples flow strongly two thousand years later.

Let us be clear. The Romans and the Jewish Sanhedrin had effectively closed the "Jesus case." The message and aims of Jesus, and his life itself, had ended in ignominious death. His prophetic voice had been muzzled. This is failure. The question is: Why had Jesus been silenced? It was because he had lived and preached God's love for humankind unflinchingly. That is why he had table fellowship with sinners, why he sought to free women and men from the tyranny of religion, why at every turn, he bore witness to the true God. In the face of the threatening opposition, he might have packed it in and gone home to Nazareth. That would have been failure indeed. They might take his life, but to his last breath he would witness. What Jesus tells us is that failure is not the last word—that is, as God views failure.

From God's point of view, there could be no question of failure in the fate of Jesus. This is what John brings out dramatically in his gospel. He undoubtedly knew the tradition behind the synoptic gospels but he chose to turn their tragedy into triumph. What is important for us in his presentation is that he understood what the others imply: Failure is not the last word. But what Mark has done is of equal importance. He has shown that a *sense* of failure, even for Jesus, is a grievous human experience.

Theology of the Cross

God is revealed with unwonted clarity in one human life and in one episode of human history. If Jesus is the image of the invisible God (see Col 1:15), the cross is the revelation of true God and true humankind. On the cross Jesus shows what it is to be human. God's Son dramatically demonstrates the radical powerlessness of the human being. He shows us that we are truly human when we accept our humanity, when we face the fact that we are not masters of our fate. The cross offers the authentic definition of what it is to be human: God's definition. There he starkly and firmly reminds us of who and what we are.

In the cross God defined the human being as creature—not to crush or humiliate, but that he might be, as Creator, wholly with his creature—to be Parent, with his child. On its own, humankind has indeed reason to fear. In God, in total dependence on God, there is no place for fear. The resurrection of Jesus makes that clear, for the raising of Jesus from death is God's endorsement of the definition of God established on the cross. It is there he defines himself against all human caricatures of him. God, in the cross, is a radical challenge to our hubris, our pride. He is the God who has entered, wholly, into rejection and humiliation. He is the God present in human life where to human eyes he is absent. He is God of humankind. He is God *for us*—all because he has made his self known to us in the Son who is "like us in all things."

NOTES

Introduction

1. This is splendidly expressed by Luke Timothy Johnson: "The identity of Jesus Christ is a mystery in the proper sense of the term. Even when it is disclosed, it remains beyond our human grasp: neither human reason nor human speech can adequately comprehend or express the truth that Paul states succinctly as, 'God was in Christ reconciling the world to himself' (2 Cor 5:19). Christians never had trouble confessing 'Jesus is Lord' (1 Cor 12:3), or recognizing at the experiential level that the Holy Spirit at work among them came from the exalted Lord Jesus (2 Cor 3:17–18), or praying to God through Jesus Christ (Rom 16:27). From the beginning, believers also affirmed both that 'God sent his Son' and that Jesus was 'born of a woman, born under the law' (Gal 4:4). The Nicene Creed was consistent with the earliest convictions and experiences concerning Jesus when it affirmed that the one who was 'God from God' was also the one 'born of the Virgin Mary' who 'suffered under Pontius Pilate.' ...The difficulty for the first Christians, as for us, lies not at the level of experience, profession, or prayer, but at the level of thought." "Human and Divine: Did Jesus Have Faith?" *Commonweal* 135 (2008): 10–16.

2. Edward Schillebeeckx, *Jesus in Our Western Culture* (London: SCM Press, 1987), 28.

3. Sandra Schneiders, *The Revelatory Text: Interpreting the New Testament as Sacred Scripture* (San Francisco: HarperSanFrancisco, 1991), 107–8.

4. John P. Meier, *A Marginal Jew: Rethinking the Historical Jesus*, vol. 1, *The Roots of the Problem and the Person* (New York: Doubleday, 1991).

Chapter 1

1. Jerome Murphy-O'Connor, *Jesus and Paul: Parallel Lives* (Collegeville, MN: Liturgical Press, Michael Glazier, 2007), 25.

2. Jerome Murphy-O'Connor, "John the Baptist and Jesus: History and Hypotheses," *New Testament Studies* 36 (1990): 359–506; *Jesus and Paul*, 40–48.

3. John P. Meier, *A Marginal Jew: Rethinking the Historical Jesus*, vol. 2, *Mentor, Message, and Miracles* (New York: Doubleday, 1994), 406f.

Chapter 2

1. Albert Nolan, *Jesus Today: A Spirituality of Radical Freedom* (Maryknoll, NY: Orbis Books, 2006), 50.

2. "To appreciate something of the impact that such a reversal must have had, we might imagine someone who goes around today telling the rich and those who have a high standard of living that they are not blessed, that in fact they are the most unfortunate. Why? Because the only way the human race can survive will be for the rich to lower their standard of living and share their wealth with others. The rich are going to find that very difficult." (Ibid., 51.)

3. Sandra Schneiders, *Written That You May Believe: Encountering Jesus in the Fourth Gospel* (New York: Crossroad, 1999), 142.

Chapter 3

1. C. H. Dodd, *The Epistle to the Romans* (London: Collins, 1959), 109–110.
2. The poignant Gethsemane passage will be treated again below (pp. 92–93). It suits both contexts admirably.
3. Schneiders, *Written That You May Believe*, 159.

Chapter 4

1. John P. Meier, *A Marginal Jew: Rethinking the Historical Jesus*, vol. 3, *Companions and Competitors* (New York: Doubleday, 2001).
2. Donald Senior, *The Passion of Jesus in the Gospel of Mark* (Wilmington, DE: Michael Glazier, 1984), 126.

BIBLIOGRAPHY

Barret, C. K. *Jesus and the Gospel Tradition*. London: SPCK, 1967.

Boff, Leonardo. *Jesus Christ Liberator: A Critical Christology for Our Time*. Maryknoll, NY: Orbis Books, 1978.

Brown, Raymond E. *The Death of the Messiah: From Gethsemane to the Grave; A Commentary on the Passion Narratives in the Four Gospels*. 2 vols. New York: Doubleday, 1994.

Dodd, C. H. *The Epistle to the Romans*. London: Collins, 1959.

Dunn, J. D. G. *Christianity in the Making*. Vol. 1, *Jesus Remembered*. Grand Rapids, MI: Eerdmans, 1998.

Dwyer, J. C. *Son of Man and Son of God: A New Language for Faith*. New York: Paulist Press, 1983.

Galilee, S. Freyne. *Jesus and the Gospels: Literary Approaches and Historical Investigations*. Dublin: Gill & Macmillan, 1988.

Harrington, Wilfrid. *The Jesus Story*. Collegeville, MN: Liturgical Press, Michael Glazier, 1991.

Jeremias, Joachim. *Jerusalem in the Time of Jesus*. London: SCM Press, 1969.

Johnson, Luke Timothy. "Human and Divine. Did Jesus Have Faith?" *Commonweal* 135 (2008): 10–16.

Loewe, W. F. "Jesus Christ," in *The New Dictionary of Theology*. Edited by J. Komonchak, M. Collins, and D. Lane, 533–43. Wilmington, DE: Michael Glazier, 1987.

Lohfink, Gerhard. *Jesus and Community*. Philadelphia: Fortress Press, 1985.

Meier, J. P. *A Marginal Jew: Rethinking the Historical Jesus*. Vol. 1, *The Roots of the Problem and the Person*. Vol. 2, *Mentor, Message, and Miracles*. Vol. 3, *Companions and Competitors*. New York: Doubleday, 1991–2001.

Meyer, B. F. *The Aims of Jesus*. London: SCM Press, 1979.

Murphy-O'Connor, Jerome. *Jesus and Paul: Parallel Lives*. Collegeville, MN: Liturgical Press, Michael Glazier, 2007.

———. "John the Baptist and Jesus: History and Hypotheses." *New Testament Studies* 36 (1990).

Nolan, Albert. *Jesus Today: A Spirituality of Radical Freedom*. Maryknoll, NY: Orbis Books, 2006.

Sanders, E. P. *Jesus and Judaism*. Philadelphia: Fortress Press, 1985.

Schillebeeckx, Edward. *God Is New Each Moment*. New York: Seabury Press, 1983.

———. *Jesus in Our Western Culture*. London: SCM Press, 1987.

Schneiders, Sandra. *The Revelatory Text: Interpreting the New Testament as Sacred Scripture*. San Francisco: HarperSanFrancisco, 1991.

———. *Written That You May Believe: Encountering Jesus in the Fourth Gospel*. New York: Crossroad, 1999.

Schüssler-Fiorenza, Elisabeth. *Jesus: Miriam's Child, Sophia's Prophet*. New York: Continuum, 1995.

Bibliography

Senior, Donald. *The Passion of Jesus in the Gospel of Mark*. Wilmington, DE: Michael Glazier, 1984.

Sobrino, Jon. *Jesus the Liberator: A Historical-Critical Reading of Jesus of Nazareth*. Maryknoll, NY: Orbis Books, 1993.

Thiessen, G. and A. Merx, *The Historical Jesus: A Comprehensive Guide*. London: SCM Press, 1998.